LIGHT FOR MY PATH

FOR
Grandparents

ILLUMINATING SELECTIONS
FROM SCRIPTURE

LIGHT FOR
MY PATH
FOR
Grandparents

ILLUMINATING SELECTIONS

FROM SCRIPTURE

BARBOUR
PUBLISHING

Previously published as *The Bible Promise Book for Grandparents*.

Unless otherwise noted, all scripture quotations are taken from the King James Version of the Bible.

Published by Barbour Publishing, P.O. Box 719, Uhrichsville, Ohio 44683, www.barbourbooks.com

Our mission is to publish and distribute inspirational products offering exceptional value and biblical encouragement to the masses.

 Member of the
Evangelical Christian
Publishers Association

Printed in the United States of America.

Contents

Introduction

*T*hy word is a lamp unto my feet,
and a light unto my path.

PSALM 119:105

Whatever the need of the moment, the answer is to be found in scripture, if we take the time to search for it. Whatever we're feeling, whatever we're suffering, whatever we're hoping—the Bible has something to say to us.

This collection of scriptures is meant to be used by you—a grandparent—as a handy reference when you need the Bible's comfort and guidance in your life. In these pages you'll find carefully selected verses that address topics like blessings, disappointment, gentleness, patience, and wisdom. In fact, more than four dozen categories are covered, arranged alphabetically for ease of use.

This book is not intended to replace regular, personal Bible study. Nor is it a replacement for a good concordance for in-depth study of a particular subject. It is, however, a quick reference to some of the key issues of life that grandparents most often face. We hope it will be an encouragement to you as you read.

Abiding in Christ

As grandparents, we have lived through years of hard work and laughter, pain and joy. Many things about our lives have changed over the years, but one thing remains constant: our God who loves us. When we abide in Him, we make Him our home, our dwelling that endures forever. "Though the earth be removed. . .the LORD of hosts is with us; the God of Jacob is our refuge" (Psalm 46:2, 7). Despite the changes time brings, if we abide in God, His love will abide with us forever.

He that dwelleth in the secret place of the most High shall abide under the shadow of the Almighty.

I will say of the LORD, He is my refuge and my fortress: my God; in him will I trust.

PSALM 91:1–2

*F*or it is impossible to be
in the presence of Jesus
and not be changed.

JOANNA WEAVER

LORD, who shall abide in thy tabernacle? who shall dwell in thy holy hill? He that walketh uprightly, and worketh righteousness, and speaketh the truth in His heart.

PSALM 15:1–2

They that trust in the LORD shall be as mount Zion, which cannot be removed, but abideth for ever.

As the mountains are round about Jerusalem, so the LORD is round about his people from henceforth even for ever.

PSALM 125:1–2

For thou hast been a shelter for me, and a strong tower from the enemy.

I will abide in thy tabernacle for ever: I will trust in the covert of thy wings. . . .

So will I sing praise unto thy name for ever.

PSALM 61:3–4, 8

If ye love me, keep my commandments.

And I will pray the Father, and he shall give you another Comforter, that he may abide with you for ever.

Even the Spirit of truth; whom the world cannot receive, because it seeth him not, neither knoweth him: but ye know him; for he dwelleth with you, and shall be in you.

I will not leave you comfortless: I will come to you.

Yet a little while, and the world seeth me no more; but ye see me: because I live, ye shall live also.

At that day ye shall know that I am in my Father, and ye in me, and I in you. . . .

If a man love me, he will keep my words: and my Father will love him, and we will come unto him, and make our abode with him.

JOHN 14:15–20, 23

But whoso keepeth his word, in him verily is the love of God perfected: hereby know we that we are in him.

He that saith he abideth in him ought himself also so to walk, even as he walked. . . .

He that saith he is in the light, and hateth his brother, is in darkness even until now.

He that loveth his brother abideth in the light, and there is none occasion of stumbling in him. . . .

But the anointing which ye have received of him abideth

in you, and ye need not that any man teach you: but as the same anointing teacheth you of all things, and is truth, and is no lie, and as it hath taught you, ye shall abide in him.

And now, little children, abide in him; that, when he shall appear, we may have confidence, and not be ashamed before him at his coming.

1 JOHN 2:5–6, 9–10, 27–28

Abide in me, and I in you. As the branch cannot bear fruit of itself, except it abide in the vine; no more can ye, except ye abide in me.

I am the vine, ye are the branches: He that abideth in me, and I in him, the same bringeth forth much fruit: for without me ye can do nothing. . . .

If ye abide in me, and my words abide in you, ye shall ask what ye will, and it shall be done unto you.

JOHN 15:4–5, 7

Lord,

I thank You for being my sure place of refuge.
Circumstances are continually changing around me,
but You remain constant.
Your love for me is evidenced by the fact that
You are always close, waiting with open arms.
Amen.

Blessings

$\mathcal{A}$s grandparents, we stand at a point in our lives where we can look back and see clearly the many blessings God has given us down through the years. God has richly blessed us and our families, and He will continue to bless us, now and forever.

Blessed be the God and Father of our Lord Jesus Christ, who hath blessed us with all spiritual blessings in heavenly places in Christ.

EPHESIANS 1:3

And I the LORD will be their God. . .and I will cause the shower to come down in his season; there shall be showers of blessing.

EZEKIEL 34:24, 26

For such as be blessed of him shall inherit the earth. . . .

I have been young, and now am old; yet have I not seen the righteous forsaken, nor his seed begging bread.

He is ever merciful, and lendeth; and his seed is blessed.

PSALM 37:22, 25–26

*O*ur prayers should be for blessings in general,
for God knows best what is good for us.

SOCRATES

The blessing of the LORD, it maketh rich, and he addeth no sorrow with it.

PROVERBS 10:22

And therefore will the LORD wait, that he may be gracious unto you, and therefore will he be exalted, that he may have mercy upon you: for the LORD is a God of judgment: blessed are all they that wait for him.

ISAIAH 30:18

Blessed is every one that feareth the LORD; that walketh in his ways.

For thou shalt eat the labour of thine hands: happy shalt thou be, and it shall be well with thee.

Thy wife shall be as a fruitful vine by the sides of thine house: thy children like olive plants round about thy table.

Behold, that thus shall the man be blessed that feareth the LORD.

The LORD shall bless thee out of Zion: and thou shalt see the good of Jerusalem all the days of thy life.

Yea, thou shalt see thy children's children, and peace upon Israel.

PSALM 128

Praise ye the LORD. Blessed is the man that feareth the LORD, that delighteth greatly in his commandments.

His seed shall be mighty upon earth: the generation of the upright shall be blessed.

Wealth and riches shall be in his house: and his righteousness endureth for ever. . . .

He shall not be afraid of evil tidings: his heart is fixed, trusting in the LORD.

PSALM 112:1–3, 7

Blessed is the man that walketh not in the counsel of the ungodly, nor standeth in the way of sinners, nor sitteth in the seat of the scornful.

But his delight is in the law of the LORD; and in his law doth he meditate day and night.

And he shall be like a tree planted by the rivers of water, that bringeth forth his fruit in his season; his leaf also shall not wither; and whatsoever he doeth shall prosper.

PSALM 1:1–3

And it shall come to pass, if thou shalt hearken diligently unto the voice of the LORD thy God, to observe and to do all his commandments which I command thee this day, that the LORD thy God will set thee on high above all nations of the earth.

And all these blessings shall come on thee, and overtake thee, if thou shalt hearken unto the voice of the LORD thy God.

Blessed shalt thou be in the city, and blessed shalt thou be in the field.

Blessed shall be the fruit of thy body, and the fruit of thy ground, and the fruit of thy cattle, the increase of thy kine, and the flocks of thy sheep.

Blessed shall be thy basket and thy store.

Blessed shalt thou be when thou comest in, and blessed shalt thou be when thou goest out.

DEUTERONOMY 28:1–6

Blessed are the poor in spirit: for theirs is the kingdom of heaven.

Blessed are they that mourn: for they shall be comforted.

Blessed are the meek: for they shall inherit the earth.

Blessed are they which do hunger and thirst after righteousness: for they shall be filled.

Blessed are the merciful: for they shall obtain mercy.

Blessed are the pure in heart: for they shall see God.

Blessed are the peacemakers: for they shall be called the children of God.

Blessed are they which are persecuted for righteousness' sake: for theirs is the kingdom of heaven.

Blessed are ye, when men shall revile you, and persecute you, and shall say all manner of evil against you falsely, for my sake.

Rejoice and be exceeding glad.

MATTHEW 5:3–12

A faithful man shall abound with blessings: but he that maketh haste to be rich shall not be innocent.

PROVERBS 28:20

Heavenly Father,
You have abundantly blessed me.
Thank You for my precious children and grandchildren.
Make me a blessing in their lives,
as well as in the lives of everyone with whom I come in
contact. Although I'm thankful for the material possessions
You've given to me,
I'm most grateful for the treasure of my family—
the only blessings I can take to heaven with me.
Amen.

Christlike Living

As grandparents, many of us have retired from the careers that once filled so much of our lives. Those professional goals that once seemed important have now dropped away. But one goal is still with us, a spiritual goal that will continue to affect the choices we make: We are called to live our lives like Christ lived His.

I am crucified with Christ: nevertheless I live; yet not I, but Christ liveth in me: and the life which I now live in the flesh I live by the faith of the Son of God, who loved me, and gave himself for me.

GALATIANS 2:20

For this cause I bow my knees unto the Father of our Lord Jesus Christ,

Of whom the whole family in heaven and earth is named,

That he would grant you, according to the riches of his glory, to be strengthened with might by his Spirit in the inner man;

That Christ may dwell in your hearts by faith; that ye, being rooted and grounded in love,

May be able to. . .know the love of Christ, which passeth knowledge, that ye might be filled with all the fulness of God.

EPHESIANS 3:14–19

*A*bove all, desire to please Christ;
dread His disapproval above everything else.

ROWLAND CROUCHER

Therefore if any man be in Christ, he is a new creature: old things are passed away; behold, all things are become new.

2 CORINTHIANS 5:17

Now thanks be unto God, which always causeth us to triumph in Christ, and maketh manifest the savour of his knowledge by us in every place.

For we are unto God a sweet savour of Christ.

2 CORINTHIANS 2:14–15

Forasmuch as ye are manifestly declared to be the epistle of Christ ministered by us, written not with ink, but with the Spirit of the living God; not in tables of stone, but in fleshy tables of the heart.

2 CORINTHIANS 3:3

Now if we be dead with Christ, we believe that we shall also live with him.

ROMANS 6:8

But God, who is rich in mercy, for his great love wherewith he loved us,

Even when we were dead in sins, hath quickened us together with Christ, (by grace ye are saved);

And hath raised us up together, and made us sit together in heavenly places in Christ Jesus.

EPHESIANS 2:4–6

As ye have therefore received Christ Jesus the Lord, so walk ye in him:

Rooted and built up in him, and stablished in the faith, as ye have been taught, abounding therein with thanksgiving.

COLOSSIANS 2:6–7

Then said Jesus unto his disciples, If any man will come after me, let him deny himself, and take up his cross, and follow me.

MATTHEW 16:24

If ye then be risen with Christ, seek those things which are above, where Christ sitteth on the right hand of God.

Set your affection on things above, not on things on the earth.

For ye are dead, and your life is hid with Christ in God.

When Christ, who is our life, shall appear, then shall ye also appear with him in glory.

COLOSSIANS 3:1–4

Dear God,
I want my life to mirror You.
I'm grateful for the new life I have in You.
Fill me with Your Spirit daily,
so that I may be an effective witness of Your love.
Amen.

Comfort

Life can be filled with troubles. We worry about our families, our children and grandchildren. We worry about our health. We worry about stretching our income to meet our financial needs. Yet how blessed we are to have a God big enough to handle all our worries! If we only allow Him, He will not fail to comfort our fearful hearts—and then we will be able to pass this holy comfort on to those around us.

Blessed be God, even the Father of our Lord Jesus Christ, the Father of mercies, and the God of all comfort;

Who comforteth us in all our tribulation, that we may be able to comfort them which are in any trouble, by the comfort wherewith we ourselves are comforted of God.

For as the sufferings of Christ abound in us, so our consolation also aboundeth by Christ.

2 CORINTHIANS 1:3–5

*A*ll you really need is the One who
promised never to leave or forsake you—
the One who said,
"Lo, I am with you always."

JONI EARECKSON TADA

But the Comforter, which is the Holy Ghost, whom the Father will send in my name, he shall teach you all things, and bring all things to your remembrance, whatsoever I have said unto you.

Peace I leave with you, my peace I give unto you: not as the world giveth, give I unto you. Let not your heart be troubled, neither let it be afraid.

JOHN 14:26–27

In the multitude of my thoughts within me thy comforts delight my soul.

PSALM 94:19

Yea, though I walk through the valley of the shadow of death, I will fear no evil: for thou art with me; thy rod and thy staff they comfort me.

PSALM 23:4

Thou, which hast shewed me great and sore troubles, shalt quicken me again, and shalt bring me up again from the depths of the earth.

Thou shalt increase my greatness, and comfort me on every side.

PSALM 71:20–21

Sing, O heavens; and be joyful, O earth; and break forth into singing, O mountains: for the LORD hath comforted his people, and will have mercy upon his afflicted.

ISAIAH 49:13

Therefore the redeemed of the LORD shall return, and come with singing unto Zion; and everlasting joy shall be upon their head: they shall obtain gladness and joy; and sorrow and mourning shall flee away.

I, even I, am he that comforteth you: who art thou, that thou shouldest be afraid of a man that shall die, and of the son of man which shall be made as grass.

ISAIAH 51:11–12

Be of good comfort; thy faith hath made thee whole.

MATTHEW 9:22

This is my comfort in my affliction: for thy word hath quickened me. . . .

Let, I pray thee, thy merciful kindness be for my comfort, according to thy word unto thy servant.

PSALM 119:50, 76

Comfort ye, comfort ye my people, saith your God.

ISAIAH 40:1

As one whom his mother comforteth, so will I comfort you; and ye shall be comforted.

ISAIAH 66:13

*F*or whatsoever things were written
aforetime were written for our learning,
that we through patience and comfort
of the scriptures might have hope.

ROMANS 15:4

And God shall wipe away all tears from their eyes; and there shall be no more death, neither sorrow, nor crying, neither shall there be any more pain: for the former things are passed away.

REVELATION 21:4

The Lord GOD will wipe away tears from off all faces.

ISAIAH 25:8

For the Lord himself shall descend from heaven with a shout, with the voice of the archangel, and with the trump of God: and the dead in Christ shall rise first:

Then we which are alive and remain shall be caught up together with them in the clouds, to meet the Lord in the air: and so shall we ever be with the Lord.

Wherefore comfort one another with these words.

1 THESSALONIANS 4:16–18

Blessed are they that mourn: for they shall be comforted

MATTHEW 5:4

And I will pray the Father, and he shall give you another Comforter, that he may abide with you for ever.

JOHN 14:16

And, lo, I am with you alway, even unto the end of the world.

MATTHEW 28:20

I will not leave you comfortless: I will come to you.

JOHN 14:18

Draw nigh to God, and he will draw nigh to you.

JAMES 4:8

Lord Jesus,
I come to You for comfort.
Even my closest friends disappoint me at times,
but You will never fail me.
You are my dearest Friend,
and I ask that You comfort me now.
Amen.

Confidence

A s we look back on our lives, we can see that down through the years God has never forsaken us. Those around us who are younger, our children and our grandchildren, should be able to gain strength from our confidence in God's faithfulness.

For thus saith the Lord GOD, the Holy One of Israel; In returning and rest shall ye be saved; in quietness and in confidence shall be your strength.

ISAIAH 30:15

According to the eternal purpose which he purposed in Christ Jesus our Lord:

In whom we have boldness and access with confidence by the faith of him.

EPHESIANS 3:11–12

Now he that hath wrought us for the selfsame thing is God, who also hath given unto us the earnest of the Spirit.

Therefore we are always confident. . . .

(For we walk by faith, not by sight):

We are confident, I say.

2 CORINTHIANS 5:5–8

*O*utlook determines outcome;
attitude determines action.

WARREN WIERSBE

For the LORD shall be thy confidence, and shall keep thy foot from being taken.

PROVERBS 3:26

Being confident of this very thing, that he which hath begun a good work in you will perform it until the day of Jesus Christ.

PHILIPPIANS 1:6

Though an host should encamp against me, my heart shall not fear: though war should rise against me, in this will I be confident. . . .

For in the time of trouble he shall hide me in his pavilion: in the secret of his tabernacle shall he hide me: he shall set me up upon a rock.

PSALM 27:3, 5

But Christ as a son over his own house; whose house are we, if we hold fast the confidence and the rejoicing of the hope firm unto the end.

HEBREWS 3:6

Dear Father,
I put my complete confidence in You.
You promise to care for me,
and I know that You will keep Your promise.
Let others be able to see my assurance in Your love and care.
Amen.

Courage

All of us are afraid sometimes. Perhaps more than anything else, it's the future that frightens us, the unknown. When we were younger, many of us assumed that nothing bad would ever happen to us, but now we know that sooner or later troubles come to everyone. It's common to feel scared—but the most frequently repeated command in the Bible is this: Be not afraid.

Be strong and of a good courage, fear not, nor be afraid of them: for the LORD thy God, he it is that doth go with thee; he will not fail thee, nor forsake thee.

DEUTERONOMY 31:6

I had fainted, unless I had believed to see the goodness of the LORD in the land of the living.

Wait on the LORD: be of good courage, and he shall strengthen thine heart: wait, I say, on the LORD.

PSALM 27:13–14

*W*hatever you do,
you need courage.
RALPH WALDO EMERSON

Jesus spake unto them, saying, Be of good cheer; it is I; be not afraid.

MATTHEW 14:27

When thou liest down, thou shalt not be afraid: yea, thou shalt lie down, and thy sleep shall be sweet.

Be not afraid of sudden fear.

PROVERBS 3:24–25

As I was with Moses, so I will be with thee: I will not fail thee, nor forsake thee.

Be strong and of a good courage.

JOSHUA 1:5–6

For God hath not given us the spirit of fear; but of power, and of love, and of a sound mind.

2 TIMOTHY 1:7

So that we may boldly say, The Lord is my helper, and I will not fear what man shall do unto me.

HEBREWS 13:6

For I the LORD thy God will hold thy right hand, saying unto thee, Fear not; I will help thee.

Fear not, thou worm Jacob, and ye men of Israel; I will help thee, saith the LORD, and thy redeemer, the Holy One of Israel.

ISAIAH 41:13–14

These things I have spoken unto you, that in me ye might have peace. In the world ye shall have tribulation: but be of good cheer: I have overcome the world.

JOHN 16:33

And now, little children, abide in him; that, when he shall appear, we may have confidence, and not be ashamed before him at his coming.

1 JOHN 2:28

The wicked flee when no man pursueth: but the righteous are bold as a lion.

PROVERBS 28:1

Be of good courage, and he shall strengthen your heart, all ye that hope in the LORD.

PSALM 31:24

Forgive me,
Lord, for the times when I take my eyes off
of You and focus on my circumstances.
I become frightened at times when I think
of the future and what it may hold for me.
But You are already there, working everything out for my best.
I give my apprehension to You.
Please give me the courage I need in the face of fear.
Amen.

Covenant

A covenant is like a legal contract, a binding agreement that cannot be broken. As Christians, we can rest in the knowledge that God has made a covenant with us that endures throughout our entire lives. He has promised to never leave us or forsake us—and He never will. What's more, His promise holds true for our children and their children, down through the generations.

I will sing of the mercies of the LORD for ever: with my mouth will I make known thy faithfulness to all generations.

For I have said, Mercy shall be built up for ever: thy faithfulness shalt thou establish in the very heavens.

I have made a covenant with my chosen. . . .

Thy seed will I establish for ever.

PSALM 89:1–4

I claim the fulfilment of God's promises,
and rightly, but that is only the human side;
the divine side is that through the promises
I recognize God's claim on me.

OSWALD CHAMBERS

But this shall be the covenant that I will make with the house of Israel; after those days, saith the LORD, I will put my law in their inward parts, and write it in their hearts; and will be their God, and they shall be my people. . . .

For they shall all know me, from the least of them unto the greatest of them, saith the LORD: for I will forgive their iniquity, and I will remember their sin no more.

JEREMIAH 31:33–34

He is the LORD our God. . . .

He hath remembered his covenant for ever, the word which he commanded to a thousand generations.

PSALM 105:7–8

As for me, this is my covenant with them, saith the LORD; my spirit that is upon thee, and my words which I have put in thy mouth, shall not depart out of thy mouth, nor out of the mouth of thy seed, nor out of the mouth of thy seed's seed, saith the LORD, from henceforth and for ever.

ISAIAH 59:21

Be strong, all ye people of the land, saith the LORD, and work: for I am with you, saith the LORD of hosts:

According to the word that I covenanted with you when ye came out of Egypt, so my spirit remaineth among you: fear ye not.

HAGGAI 2:4–5

Know therefore that the LORD thy God, he is God, the faithful God, which keepeth covenant and mercy with them that love him and keep his commandments to a thousand generations.

DEUTERONOMY 7:9

Dear Father,

*I want to be a person of my word
so that my family can follow my example.
Thank You for keeping Your promises to us.
I take comfort in the fact that Your Word will never fail.
Amen.*

Death

*F*or those of us who know Christ, death need not be a frightening and tragic event. Of course, we all feel nervous of the unknown—but God's Word promises that Christ has conquered death's darkness, leaving only a wonderful door that leads us into God's presence.

Let not your heart be troubled: ye believe in God, believe also in me.

In my Father's house are many mansions: if it were not so, I would have told you. I go to prepare a place for you.

JOHN 14:1–2

For now we see through a glass, darkly; but then face to face: now I know in part; but then shall I know even as also I am known.

1 CORINTHIANS 13:12

*W*hen you were born,
you cried and everybody else was happy.
The only question that matters is this:
When you die,
will you be happy when everybody else is crying?
TONY CAMPOLO

And God shall wipe away all tears from their eyes; and there shall be no more death, neither sorrow, nor crying, neither shall there be any more pain: for the former things are passed away.

REVELATION 21:4

We shall be like him; for we shall see him as he is.

1 JOHN 3:2

If in this life only we have hope in Christ, we are of all men most miserable.

But now is Christ risen from the dead, and become the firstfruits of them that slept. . . .

For as in Adam all die, even so in Christ shall all be made alive. . . .

For he must reign, till he hath put all enemies under his feet.

The last enemy that shall be destroyed is death. . . .

For this corruptible must put on incorruption, and this mortal must put on immortality.

So when this corruptible shall have put on incorruption, and this mortal shall have put on immortality, then shall be brought to pass the saying that is written, Death is swallowed up in victory.

O death, where is thy sting? O grave, where is thy victory?

1 CORINTHIANS 15:19–20, 22, 25–26, 53–55

But I would not have you to be ignorant, brethren, concerning them which are asleep, that ye sorrow not, even as others which have no hope.

For if we believe that Jesus died and rose again, even so them also which sleep in Jesus will God bring with him.

1 THESSALONIANS 4:13–14

Ye have in heaven a better and an enduring substance.

HEBREWS 10:34

For whether we live, we live unto the Lord; and whether we die, we die unto the Lord: whether we live therefore, or die, we are the Lord's.

ROMANS 14:8

Whilst we are at home in the body, we are absent from the Lord: . . .

We are. . .willing rather to be absent from the body, and to be present with the Lord.

2 CORINTHIANS 5:6, 8

So shall we ever be with the Lord.

Wherefore comfort one another with these words.

1 THESSALONIANS 4:17–18

And I saw a new heaven and a new earth: for the first heaven and the first earth were passed away. . . .

REVELATION 21:1

Thank You,

Lord, for being close to me even when death is near.
Please calm any fears I may have about dying,
and help me to dwell on the joy that I will experience
when I enter Your presence.
I long to be with You,
worshiping You throughout eternity.
Amen.

Diligence

Some might think that at this point in our lives we can sit back and rest on our laurels. After all, we've worked hard all our lives, and now we should be able to take it easy, in our spiritual lives as well as in our physical lives. Even at this stage of our lives, though, God calls us to be diligent. The dictionary defines *diligence* as "steady, earnest, and energetic effort"—and as Christ's followers, we must continue steadily on our Christian walk, seeking God's will in our lives with earnest effort.

And thou shalt love the LORD thy God with all thine heart, and with all thy soul, and with all thy might.

And these words, which I command thee this day, shall be in thine heart:

And thou shalt teach them diligently unto thy children, and shalt talk of them when thou sittest in thine house, and when thou walkest by the way, and when thou liest down, and when thou risest up.

DEUTERONOMY 6:5–7

I expect to pass through this world but once.

Any good therefore that I can do,

or any kindness or abilities

that I can show to any fellow creature,

let me do it now.

Let me not defer it or neglect it,

for I shall not pass this way again.

WILLIAM PENN

Wherefore, beloved. . .be diligent that ye may be found of him in peace, without spot, and blameless.

2 PETER 3:14

Therefore, as ye abound in every thing, in faith, and utterance, and knowledge, and in all diligence, and in your love to us, see that ye about in this grace also.

2 CORINTHIANS 8:7

The soul of the sluggard desireth, and hath nothing: but the soul of the diligent shall be made fat.

PROVERBS 13:4

But take diligent heed to do the commandment and the law, which Moses the servant of the LORD charged you, to love the LORD your God, and to walk in all his ways, and to keep his commandments, and to cleave unto him, and to serve him with all your heart and with all your soul.

JOSHUA 22:5

And beside this, giving all diligence, add to your faith virtue; and to virtue knowledge;

And to knowledge temperance; and to temperance patience; and to patience godliness;

And to godliness brotherly kindness; and to brotherly kindness charity.

For if these things be in you, and abound, they make you that ye shall neither be barren nor unfruitful in the knowledge of our Lord Jesus Christ.

2 PETER 1:5–8

Thou hast commanded us to keep thy precepts diligently. . . . Then shall I not be ashamed.

PSALM 119:4, 6

Follow peace with all men, and holiness, without which no man shall see the Lord:

Looking diligently lest any man fail of the grace of God; lest any root of bitterness springing up trouble you, and thereby many be defiled.

HEBREWS 12:14–15

Keep thy heart with all diligence; for out of it are the issues of life.

PROVERBS 4:23

Whatsoever is commanded by the God of heaven, let it be diligently done for the house of the God of heaven.

EZRA 7:23

The thoughts of the diligent tend only to plenteousness; but of every one that is hasty only to want.

PROVERBS 21:5

Heavenly Father,
I have worked hard throughout my life,
reaching toward the accomplishment of my goals.
I don't ever want to cease making progress,
especially in growing in my Christian life.
You are my coach—
my trainer and encourager as I
run the race You have for me.
Amen.

Disappointment

$\mathcal{W}$e have such high hopes for our children and our grandchildren, and even for ourselves. Sometimes, though, life doesn't turn out the way we had hoped. When disappointments come, how good it is to know that we can cast our burdens on the Lord—and He will sustain us (Psalm 55:22).

Why art thou cast down, O my soul? and why art thou disquieted in me? hope thou in God: for I shall yet praise him for the help of his countenance.

PSALM 42:5

*T*he close communion that the Lord desires
and is willing to experience with us is
something we can count on,
even if everyone else abandons us.

CHARLES STANLEY

Behold, I have refined thee, but not with silver; I have chosen thee in the furnace of affliction.

ISAIAH 48:10

Although the fig tree shall not blossom, neither shall fruit be in the vines; the labour of the olive shall fail, and the fields shall yield no meat; the flock shall be cut off from the fold, and there shall be no herd in the stalls:

Yet I will rejoice in the LORD, I will joy in the God of my salvation.

HABAKKUK 3:17–18

I have learned, in whatsoever state I am. . .to be content.

PHILIPPIANS 4:11

Tribulation worketh patience.

ROMANS 5:3

O Lord,
It's been an awful day.
Help me not to let my feelings be a barometer
of my spiritual status.
Let me not go on feelings but on the facts. . .
that You forgive and that You love me unconditionally.
Amen.

Discipline

We don't always think of discipline as a positive thing. In fact, most of us would rather avoid it. Just like our grandchildren, we'd rather do what we want, when we want. But actually, for grandparents as well as children, discipline is the way we all grow and learn.

When we are judged, we are chastened of the Lord, that we should not be condemned with the world.

1 CORINTHIANS 11:32

My son, despise not the chastening of the LORD; neither be weary of his correction:

For whom the LORD loveth he correcteth; even as a father the son in whom he delighteth.

PROVERBS 3:11–12

*G*od has to punish His children
from time to time,
and it is the very demonstration of His love.

ELISABETH ELLIOT

Blessed is the man whom thou chastenest, O LORD, and teachest him out of thy law;

That thou mayest give him rest from the days of adversity.

PSALM 94:12–13

Thou shalt also consider in thine heart, that, as a man chasteneth his son, so the LORD thy God chasteneth thee.

DEUTERONOMY 8:5

Behold, happy is the man whom God correcteth: therefore despise not thou the chastening of the Almighty.

For he maketh sore, and bindeth up: he woundeth, and his hands make whole.

JOB 5:17–18

As many as I love, I rebuke and chasten.

REVELATION 3:19

O LORD, rebuke me not in thine anger, neither chasten me in thy hot displeasure.

PSALM 6:1

My son, despise not thou the chastening of the Lord, nor faint when thou art rebuked of him:

For whom the Lord loveth he chasteneth, and scourgeth every son whom he receiveth.

If ye endure chastening, God dealeth with you as with sons; for what son is he whom the father chasteneth not? . . .

Now no chastening for the present seemeth to be joyous, but grievous: nevertheless afterward it yieldeth the peaceable fruit of righteousness unto them which are exercised thereby.

HEBREWS 12:5–7, 11

Dear God,
Although discipline hurts,
I thank You for loving me enough to correct me
when I make the wrong choices.
Please help me to accept Your discipline with grace,
so that I may not only grow in my Christian life,
but also be an example to my family.
Amen.

Encouragement

As a grandparent, your children and grandchildren will look to you for guidance and encouragement in their lives. Seek the treasures in God's Word, and you'll always point them to the right path.

But exhort one another daily, while it is called To day; lest any of you be hardened through the deceitfulness of sin.

HEBREWS 3:13

Confirming the souls of the disciples, and exhorting them to continue in the faith, and that we must through much tribulation enter into the kingdom of God.

ACTS 14:22

*W*hen someone does something good, applaud!
You will make two people happy.

SAMUEL GOLDWYN

Holding fast the faithful word as he hath been taught, that he may be able by sound doctrine both to exhort and to convince the gainsayers.

TITUS 1:9

Not forsaking the assembling of ourselves together, as the manner of some is; but exhorting one another: and so much the more, as ye see the day approaching.

HEBREWS 10:25

And whether we be afflicted, it is for your consolation and salvation, which is effectual in the enduring of the same sufferings which we also suffer: or whether we be comforted, it is for your consolation and salvation.

2 CORINTHIANS 1:6

I can do all things through Christ which strengtheneth me.

PHILIPPIANS 4:13

Therefore, brethren, stand fast, and hold the traditions which ye have been taught, whether by word, or our epistle.

Now our Lord Jesus Christ himself, and God, even our Father, which hath loved us, and hath given us everlasting consolation and good hope through grace,

Comfort your hearts, and stablish you in every good word and work.

2 THESSALONIANS 2:15–17

All scripture is given by inspiration of God, and is profitable for doctrine, for reproof, for correction, for instruction in righteousness.

2 TIMOTHY 3:16

He giveth power to the faint; and to them that have no might he increaseth strength.

ISAIAH 40:29

Wherefore comfort yourselves together, and edify one another, even as also ye do.

1 THESSALONIANS 5:11

And when they bring you unto the synagogues, and unto magistrates, and powers, take ye no thought how or what thing ye shall answer, or what ye shall say:

For the Holy Ghost shall teach you in the same hour what ye ought to say.

LUKE 12:11–12

Brethren, if any of you do err from the truth, and one convert him;

Let him know, that he which converteth the sinner from the error of his way shall save a soul from death, and shall hide a multitude of sins.

JAMES 5:19–20

Ye are witnesses, and God also, how holily and justly and unblameably we behaved ourselves among you that believe:

As ye know how we exhorted and comforted and charged every one of you, as a father doth his children,

That ye would walk worthy of God, who hath called you unto his kingdom and glory.

For this cause also thank we God without ceasing, because, when ye received the word of God which ye heard of us, ye received it not as the word of men, but as it is in truth, the word of God, which effectually worketh also in you that believe.

1 THESSALONIANS 2:10–13

Bear ye one another's burdens, and so fulfil the law of Christ.

GALATIANS 6:2

Look not every man on his own things, but every man also on the things of others.

Dear Lord,
Thank you for Your Word that holds
an abundance of encouragement for Your children.
As I interact with my family, Lord,
may I hold Your Word in my heart
and reflect Your loving presence.
Help me to guide and encourage
my family with wisdom.
Amen.

Failure

A s we look back on our lives, we don't always feel good about everything. Some things we hoped to accomplish never came about. Some things have turned out differently than we hoped. But remember, when our eyes are focused on our own failures, then we have lost sight of Christ, the One who is able with His grace to transform even our failures. Oh, we still have to deal with the consequences of our actions. But when we place our failures in God's hands, then He will work all things together for good (Romans 8:28)—and we are free to forget the past and turn our eyes heavenward.

For my life is spent with grief, and my years with sighing: my strength faileth because of mine iniquity, and my bones are consumed.

PSALM 31:10

*O*ur greatest glory is not in never failing,
but in rising up every time we fail.
RALPH WALDO EMERSON

The steps of a good man are ordered by the LORD: and he delighteth in his way.

Though he fall, he shall not be utterly cast down: for the LORD upholdeth him with his hand.

PSALM 37:23–24

Wherefore seeing we also are compassed about with so great a cloud of witnesses, let us lay aside every weight, and the sin which doth so easily beset us, and let us run with patience the race that is set before us,

Looking unto Jesus the author and finisher of our faith; who for the joy that was set before him endured the cross, despising the shame, and is set down at the right hand of the throne of God.

HEBREWS 12:1–2

For mine iniquities are gone over mine head: as an heavy burden they are too heavy for me.

My wounds stink and are corrupt because of my foolishness.

I am troubled; I am bowed down greatly; I go mourning all the day long. . . .

Lord, all my desire is before thee; and my groaning is not hid from thee. . . .

For in thee, O LORD, do I hope: thou wilt hear, O Lord my God.

For I said, Hear me, lest otherwise they should rejoice over me: when my foot slippeth, they magnify themselves against me.

For I am ready to halt, and my sorrow is continually before me.

For I will declare mine iniquity; I will be sorry for my sin. . . . Forsake me not, O LORD: O my God, be not far from me. Make haste to help me, O Lord my salvation.

PSALM 38:4–6, 9, 15–18, 21–22

Lord Jesus,
I don't want to live a life of regret for past failures.
You don't demand perfection,
but You do require obedience.
For the times the failure is due to sin,
help me to accept the fact that I'm forgiven,
and that You have erased it from Your memory.
When the failure has been a result of poor planning,
help me to learn a lesson so that I
won't fail in that area again.
Amen.

Faithfulness

*O*ur God is a faithful God. Through all the changes and uncertainties that life brings, we can rely on God. He will never leave us nor forsake us, and He will remain faithful to our children and grandchildren, and to their children and grandchildren.

For ever, O LORD, thy word is settled in heaven.

Thy faithfulness is unto all generations: thou hast established the earth, and it abideth.

PSALM 119:89–90

O LORD, thou art my God; I will exalt thee, I will praise thy name; for thou hast done wonderful things; thy counsels of old are faithfulness and truth.

ISAIAH 25:1

*Y*our heavenly Father is too good to be unkind
and too wise to make mistakes.

CHARLES SPURGEON

I pray God your whole spirit and soul and body be preserved blameless unto the coming of our Lord Jesus Christ.

Faithful is he that calleth you, who also will do it.

1 THESSALONIANS 5:23–24

If we believe not, yet he abideth faithful: he cannot deny himself.

2 TIMOTHY 2:13

A faithful man shall abound with blessings: but he that maketh haste to be rich shall not be innocent.

PROVERBS 28:20

Let us hold fast the profession of our faith without wavering; (for he is faithful that promised).

HEBREWS 10:23

It is of the LORD's mercies that we are not consumed, because his compassions fail not.

They are new every morning: great is thy faithfulness.

LAMENTATIONS 3:22–23

Thy mercy, O LORD, is in the heavens; and thy faithfulness reacheth unto the clouds.

PSALM 36:5

I will sing of the mercies of the LORD for ever: with my mouth will I make known thy faithfulness to all generations.

For I have said, Mercy shall be built up for ever: thy faithfulness shalt thou establish in the very heavens. . . .

And the heavens shall praise thy wonders, O LORD: thy faithfulness also in the congregation of the saints.

PSALM 89:1–2, 5

God is not a man, that he should lie; neither the son of man, that he should repent: hath he said, and shall he not do it? or hath he spoken, and shall he not make it good?

NUMBERS 23:19

Know therefore that the LORD thy God, he is God, the faithful God, which keepeth covenant and mercy with them that love him and keep his commandments to a thousand generations.

DEUTERONOMY 7:9

Thank You,
Jesus, that You have not and will never change.
There is nothing else in my life that is as certain.
I am grateful that You will never leave me—
You will always be with me throughout my life,
and then will take me home to live in heaven with You.
I love You, Lord!
Amen.

Financial Worries

*D*uring our retirement years, living on a fixed income is not always easy. Our worries about money can seem overwhelming at times—but the Bible promises us that our times are in God's hands (Psalm 31:15), and we can rely on Him to provide for us.

I know both how to be abased, and I know how to abound: every where and in all things I am instructed both to be full and to be hungry, both to abound and to suffer need.

I can do all things through Christ which strengtheneth me.

PHILIPPIANS 4:12–13

*N*ever spend your money before you have it.

THOMAS JEFFERSON

Be careful for nothing; but in every thing by prayer and supplication with thanksgiving let your requests be made known unto God.

And the peace of God, which passeth understanding, shall keep your hearts and minds through Christ Jesus.

PHILIPPIANS 4:6–7

Why art thou cast down, O my soul? and why art thou disquieted in me? hope thou in God.

PSALM 42:5

Therefore I say unto you, Take no thought for your life, what ye shall eat; neither for the body, what ye shall put on.

The life is more than meat, and the body is more than raiment.

Consider the ravens: for they neither sow nor reap; which neither have storehouse nor barn; and God feedeth them: how much more are ye better than the fowls?

And which of you with taking thought can add to his stature one cubit?

If ye then be not able to do that thing which is least, why take ye thought for the rest?

Consider the lilies how they grow: they toil not, they spin not; and yet I say unto you, that Solomon in all his glory was not arrayed like one of these.

If then God so clothe the grass. . .how much more will he clothe you, O ye of little faith? . . .

Seek ye the kingdom of God; and all these things shall be added unto you.

Fear not, little flock; for it is your Father's good pleasure to give you the kingdom.

LUKE 12:22–28, 31–32

Dear Lord,

Remind me that my finances are in Your hand.
I've spent my lifetime saving my money,
striving to be a good steward of what You've provided.
Help me to manage my funds responsibly,
and take away my worry regarding future expenses.
Let me invest faith in the eternal
and be ever mindful of the riches I have in You.
Amen.

Forgiveness

We're not always treated the way we want to be. Children and grandchildren are often busy and don't have as much time for us as we'd like. Over the years, friends and loved ones have failed us in many different ways, and it's easy to hold a grudge. But God calls us to forgive each other, just as He has forgiven us for the many times we've failed Him.

Then came Peter to him, and said, Lord, how oft shall my brother sin against me, and I forgive him? till seven times?

Jesus saith unto him, I say not unto thee, Until seven times: but, Until seventy times seven.

MATTHEW 18:21–22

And when ye stand praying, forgive, if ye have ought against any: that your Father also which is in heaven may forgive you your trespasses.

MARK 11:25

*F*orgiveness is
the oil of relationships.
JOSH MCDOWELL

And be ye kind one to another, tenderhearted, forgiving one another, even as God for Christ's sake hath forgiven you.

EPHESIANS 4:32

Take heed to yourselves: If thy brother trespass against thee, rebuke him; and if he repent, forgive him.

LUKE 17:3

Be ye therefore merciful, as your Father also is merciful.

Judge not, and ye shall not be judged: condemn not, and ye shall not be condemned: forgive, and ye shall be forgiven.

LUKE 6:36–37

And forgive us our debts, as we forgive our debtors. . . .

For if ye forgive men their trespasses, your heavenly Father will also forgive you:

But if ye forgive not men their trespasses, neither will your Father forgive your trespasses.

MATTHEW 6:12, 14–15

Put on therefore, as the elect of God, holy and beloved, bowels of mercies, kindness, humbleness of mind, meekness, longsuffering;

Forbearing one another, and forgiving one another, if any man have a quarrel against any: even as Christ forgave you, so also do ye.

COLOSSIANS 3:12–13

And forgive us our sins; for we also forgive every one that is indebted to us. And lead us not into temptation; but deliver us from evil.

LUKE 11:4

The discretion of a man deferreth his anger; and it is his glory to pass over a transgression.

PROVERBS 19:11

But I say unto you, That ye resist not evil: but whosoever shall smite thee on thy right cheek, turn to him the other also.

And if any man will sue thee at the law, and take away thy coat, let him have thy cloke also.

And whosoever shall compel thee to go a mile, go with him twain.

MATTHEW 5:39–41

If my people, which are called by my name, shall humble themselves, and pray, and seek my face, and turn from their wicked ways; then will I hear from heaven, and will forgive their sin, and will heal their land.

2 CHRONICLES 7:14

For thou, Lord, art good, and ready to forgive; and plenteous in mercy unto all them that call upon thee.

PSALM 86:5

Father,
When I wonder if You can ever forgive me,
in a sense I'm saying You're not big enough.
Help me to remember that our sins have been cast
into the sea and that You've posted a
NO FISHING ALLOWED sign.
Amen.

Friendship

We form and build many friendships throughout our lives. . .but none are as sweet and lasting as those built with our grandchildren.

Iron sharpeneth iron; so a man sharpeneth the countenance
of his friend.

PROVERBS 27:17

*O*h, the comfort,
the inexpressible comfort of
feeling safe with a person;
having neither to weigh thoughts nor to
measure words but to pour them all out,
just as it is,
chaff and grain together,
knowing that a faithful hand
will take and sift them,
keeping what is worth keeping,
and then, with the breath of kindness,
blow the rest away.

GEORGE ELIOT

A man that hath friends must shew himself friendly: and there is a friend that sticketh closer than a brother.

PROVERBS 18:24

To him that is afflicted pity should be shewed from his friend; but he forsaketh the fear of the Almighty.

JOB 6:14

Which of you shall have a friend, and shall go unto him at midnight, and say unto him, Friend, lend me three loaves;

For a friend of mine in his journey is come to me, and I have nothing to set before him?

And he from within shall answer and say. . .I cannot rise and give thee.

I say unto you, Though he will not rise and give him, because he is his friend, yet because of his importunity he will rise and give him as many as he needeth.

LUKE 11:5–8

A friend loveth at all times.

PROVERBS 17:17

Faithful are the wounds of a friend.

PROVERBS 27:6

Lord,
In our world of instant everything,
help me to remember that
relationships take time.
Amen.

Generosity

We who are older have a wealth of riches to share with our families and others around us. Our riches may not be material; instead, they may be our time, our wisdom, our ability to listen, or simply our love. Whatever we have much of, God calls us to share it with those in need—and then He, too, will share with us His abundance.

Is not this the fast I have chosen? . . .

Is it not to deal thy bread to the hungry, and that thou bring the poor that are cast out to thy house? when thou seest the naked, that thou cover him; and that thou hide not thyself from thine own flesh? . . .

And if thou draw out thy soul to the hungry, and satisfy the afflicted soul; then shall thy light rise in obscurity, and thy darkness be as the noon day:

And the LORD shall guide thee continually, and satisfy thy soul in drought, and make fat thy bones: and thou shalt be like a watered garden, and like a spring of water, whose waters fail not. . . .

Thou shalt raise up the foundations of many generations; and thou shalt be called, The repairer of the breach, The restorer of paths to dwell in.

ISAIAH 58:6–7, 10–12

*G*ive what you have.

To someone,

it may be better than you dare to think.

HENRY WADSWORTH LONGFELLOW

Give, and it shall be given unto you; good measure, pressed down, and shaken together, and running over, shall men give into your bosom. For with the same measure that ye mete withal it shall be measured to you again.

LUKE 6:38

But when thou makest a feast, call the poor, the maimed, the lame, the blind:

And thou shalt be blessed; for they cannot recompense thee: for thou shalt be recompensed at the resurrection of the just.

LUKE 14:13–14

He that despiseth his neighbour sinneth: but he that hath mercy on the poor, happy is he.

PROVERBS 14:21

Charge them that are rich in this world, that they be not highminded, nor trust in uncertain riches, but in the living God, who giveth us richly all things to enjoy;

That they do good, that they be rich in good works, ready to distribute, willing to communicate.

1 TIMOTHY 6:17–18

A good man sheweth favour, and lendeth. . . .

He hath dispersed, he hath given to the poor; his righteousness endureth for ever; his horn shall be exalted with honour.

PSALM 112:5, 9

He that hath pity upon the poor lendeth unto the LORD; and that which he hath given will he pay him again.

PROVERBS 19:17

He that giveth unto the poor shall not lack: but he that hideth his eyes shall have many a curse.

PROVERBS 28:27

He answereth and saith unto them, He that hath two coats, let him impart to him that hath none; and he that hath meat, let him do likewise.

LUKE 3:11

Sell that ye have, and give alms; provide yourselves bags which wax not old, a treasure in the heavens that faileth not, where no thief approacheth, neither moth corrupteth.

For where your treasure is, there will your heart be also.

LUKE 12:33–34

Withhold not good from them to whom it is due, when it is in the power of thine hand to do it.

Say not unto thy neighbour, Go, and come again, and tomorrow I will give; when thou hast it by thee.

PROVERBS 3:27–28

Every man shall give as he is able, according to the blessing of the LORD thy God which he hath given thee.

DEUTERONOMY 16:17

Blessed is he that considereth the poor: the LORD will deliver him in time of trouble.

The LORD will preserve him, and keep him alive; and he shall be blessed upon the earth: and thou wilt not deliver him unto the will of his enemies.

PSALM 41:1–2

Let him give; not grudgingly, or of necessity: for God loveth a cheerful giver.

And God is able to make all grace abound toward you; that ye, always having all sufficiency in all things, may abound to every good work. . . .

Being enriched in every thing to all bountifulness, which causeth through us thanksgiving to God.

2 CORINTHIANS 9:7–8, 11

Dear Lord,
I am so grateful for all You've given to me.
You have blessed me with not only material possessions,
but also with unique talents that I can share with others.
Make me aware of those who need assistance,
so that I can share my time in helping
or even just listening when they need to talk.
My treasure and abilities are Yours, Lord.
I want to use them to benefit others.
Amen.

Gentleness

We are all impatient with others. When we don't feel well, we're often cranky; when we know a better way to do things and no one pays attention to our advice, we frequently speak harshly; and when our feelings are hurt, it's all too easy to snap. If we let the Holy Spirit work in our lives, however, He will produce His fruit—one of which is gentleness.

But foolish and unlearned questions avoid, knowing that they do gender strifes.

And the servant of the Lord must not strive; but be gentle unto all men, apt to teach, patient,

In meekness instructing those that oppose themselves; if God peradventure will give them repentance to the acknowledging of the truth.

2 TIMOTHY 2:23–25

*H*ow much of a calm and gentle spirit
you achieve, then, will depend on how regularly
and consistently, persistently and obediently,
you partake of the Word of God,
your spiritual food.

SHIRLEY RICE

Speak evil of no man, to be no brawlers, but gentle, shewing all meekness unto all men.

TITUS 3:2

The meek shall eat and be satisfied: they shall praise the LORD that seek him: your heart shall live for ever.

PSALM 22:26

Seek ye the LORD, all ye meek of the earth, which have wrought his judgment; seek righteousness, seek meekness.

ZEPHANIAH 2:3

Take my yoke upon you, and learn of me; for I am meek and lowly in heart: and ye shall find rest unto your souls

MATTHEW 11:29

But the fruit of the Spirit is love, joy, peace, longsuffering, gentleness, goodness, faith,

Meekness, temperance: against such there is no law.

GALATIANS 5:22–23

Who is a wise man and endued with knowledge among you? let him shew out of a good conversation his works with meekness of wisdom. . . .

The wisdom that is from above is first pure, then peaceable, gentle, and easy to be intreated, full of mercy and good fruits, without partiality, and without hypocrisy.

And the fruit of righteousness is sown in peace of them that make peace.

JAMES 3:13, 17–18

The meek will he guide in judgment: and the meek will he teach his way.

PSALM 25:9

But the meek shall inherit the earth; and shall delight themselves in the abundance of peace.

PSALM 37:11

For the LORD taketh pleasure in his people: he will beautify the meek with salvation.

PSALM 149:4

Follow after righteousness, godliness, faith, love, patience, meekness.

1 TIMOTHY 6:11

The LORD lifteth up the meek.

PSALM 147:6

Lord,
Sometimes when demands or expectations
are too great for me,
I become impatient.
I want to react with a gentle spirit,
for when I do,
the situation improves,
as well as my attitude.
Ripen the fruit of gentleness in my life.
Amen.

Grandchildren

$\mathcal{T}$he birth of a grandchild is one of life's greatest joys. How God blesses us with these precious children!

Lo, children are an heritage of the LORD.

PSALM 127:3

For this child I have prayed; and the LORD hath given me my petition which I asked of him.

1 SAMUEL 1:27

Thy children like olive plants round about thy table.

PSALM 128:3

*H*appy is the grandparent who
can share adventures with a grandchild,
walking a nature trail, exploring a museum,
or sitting together in church. . . .
Reaching out to one's grandchildren
and great-grandchildren can renew us, and them.

JOHN GILLIES

Whosoever shall receive one of such children in my name, receiveth me: and whosoever shall receive me, receiveth not me, but him that sent me.

MARK 9:37

Suffer the little children to come unto me, and forbid them not: for of such is the kingdom of God.

Mark 10:14

For I say unto you, That in heaven their angels do always behold the face of my Father which is in heaven.

Matthew 18:10

Dear God,

Thank You for blessing me with such a beautiful grandchild.
I anticipate the play times,
the conversations on the telephone,
and each birthday celebration.
But I most sincerely want to be a tool in Your hand,
cultivating this child's mind in You.
Bless my precious grandchild, I pray.
Amen.

Guidance

*I*n this phase of our lives, we need God's guidance just as much as ever. Should we move into a smaller house now that our children are grown—or keep the familiar home we love so much? Should we stay close to friends and family—or move south where the winters are easier? Should we give our children some much-needed advice—or should we keep our opinions to ourselves? God has the answers to all these questions, and as we seek His will, He will show us the ways we should go.

He led them forth by the right way.

PSALM 107:7

[God] made his own people to go forth like sheep, and guided them in the wilderness like a flock.

And he led them on safely, so that they feared not.

PSALM 78:52–53

For this God is our God for ever and ever: he will be our guide even unto death.

PSALM 48:14

*W*rite down the advice of
him who loves you,
though you like it not at the present.

ENGLISH PROVERB

Shew me thy ways, O LORD; teach me thy paths.

Lead me in thy truth, and teach me: for thou art the God of my salvation; on thee do I wait all the day.

PSALM 25:4–5

O send out thy light and thy truth: let them lead me; let them bring me unto thy holy hill, and to thy tabernacles.

PSALM 43:3

For the Lamb which is in the midst of the throne shall feed them, and shall lead them unto living fountains of waters.

REVELATION 7:17

For thou art my rock and my fortress; therefore for thy name's sake lead me, and guide me.

PSALM 31:3

He leadeth me beside the still waters.

He restoreth my soul: he leadeth me in the paths of righteousness for his name's sake.

PSALM 23:2–3

Lead me, O LORD, in thy righteousness. . .make thy way straight before my face.

PSALM 5:8

He found him in a desert land, and in the waste howling wilderness; he led him about, he instructed him, he kept him as the apple of his eye.

As an eagle stirreth up her nest, fluttereth over her young, spreadeth abroad her wings, taketh them, beareth them on her wings:

So the LORD alone did lead him.

DEUTERONOMY 32:10–12

Teach me thy way, O LORD, and lead me in a plain path.

PSALM 27:11

And even to your old age I am he; and even to hoar hairs will I carry you: I have made, and I will bear; even I will carry, and will deliver you.

ISAIAH 46:4

He that hath mercy on them shall lead them, even by the springs of water shall he guide them.

ISAIAH 49:10

I have seen his ways, and will heal him: I will lead him also, and restore comforts unto him.

ISAIAH 57:18

The LORD shall guide thee continually, and satisfy thy soul in drought, and make fat thy bones: and thou shalt be like a watered garden, and like a spring of water, whose waters fail not.

ISAIAH 58:11

Howbeit when he, the Spirit of truth, is come, he will guide you into all truth.

JOHN 16:13

In all thy ways acknowledge him, and he shall direct thy paths.

PROVERBS 3:6

Heavenly Father,
I seek Your will in the unknowns of my life.
I want to be listening for Your still, small voice.
Quiet me, so that I can focus on Your direction.
Amen.

Healing

As we get older, our bodies seem to fail us more and more often. The Bible assures us we can turn to God for healing. Sometimes, though, He chooses not to deliver us from a physical affliction—but even then, He will still bring us to spiritual and eternal health.

Bless the LORD, O my soul, and forget not all his benefits:

Who forgiveth all thine iniquities; who healeth all thy diseases;

Who redeemeth thy life from destruction; who crowneth thee with lovingkindness and tender mercies;

Who satisfieth thy mouth with good things; so that thy youth is renewed like the eagle's.

PSALM 103:2–5

*O*ne of the main things
Jesus wants to be to us is
the forgiver of our sins
and the healer of our bodies.
Let's lay hold of
the health and healing He has. . .
by praying for it
even before the need arises.

STORMIE O'MARTIAN

Heal me, O LORD, and I shall be healed; save me, and I shall be saved: for thou art my praise.

JEREMIAH 17:14

Come, and let us return unto the LORD: for he hath torn, and he will heal us; he hath smitten, and he will bind us up.

HOSEA 6:1

For I will restore health unto thee, and I will heal thee of thy wounds, saith the LORD.

JEREMIAH 30:17

I will heal their backsliding, I will love them freely: for mine anger is turned away from him.

HOSEA 14:4

But unto you that fear my name shall the Sun of righteousness arise with healing in his wings; and ye shall go forth, and grow up as calves of the stall.

MALACHI 4:2

O LORD my God, I cried unto thee, and thou hast healed me.
O LORD, thou hast brought up my soul from the grave: thou hast kept me alive.

PSALM 30:2–3

And. . .if thou wilt diligently hearken to the voice of the LORD thy God, and wilt do that which is right in his sight, and wilt give ear to his commandments, and keep all his statutes, I will put none of these diseases upon thee. . .for I am the LORD that healeth thee.

EXODUS 15:26

And Jesus saith unto him, I will come and heal him.

MATTHEW 8:7

Is any among you afflicted? let him pray. Is any merry? let him sing psalms.

Is any sick among you? let him call for the elders of the church; and let them pray over him, anointing him with oil in the name of the Lord:

And the prayer of faith shall save the sick, and the Lord shall raise him up; and if he have committed sins, they shall be forgiven him.

JAMES 5:13–15

Thank You,
Father, for being my Great Physician.
I'm grateful for doctors who are able to help me,
but acknowledge that You are the One
who ultimately heals me.
I look forward with joy to being in Your presence,
where I will no longer suffer any pain.
Amen.

Heritage

These days, people are interested in their ancestry. Researching our heritage is a popular thing to do, and as grandparents, we are in a wonderful position to pass our heritage on to our children and grandchildren. As valuable as our earthly heritage is, however, how much more valuable is the heavenly heritage we have in Christ! The inheritance handed down to us from God through Christ will last for eternity.

The LORD is the portion of mine inheritance and of my cup: thou maintainest my lot.

The lines are fallen unto me in pleasant places; yea, I have a goodly heritage.

PSALM 16:5–6

I will abide in thy tabernacle for ever: I will trust in the covert of thy wings. . . .

For thou, O God. . .hast given me the heritage of those that fear thy name.

PSALM 61:4–5

*T*o forget one's ancestors is
to be a brook without a source,
a tree without a root.

CHINESE PROVERB

The wise shall inherit glory.

PROVERBS 3:35

Then shall the King say unto them on his right hand, Come, ye blessed of my Father, inherit the kingdom prepared for you from the foundation of the world.

MATTHEW 25:34

And every one that hath forsaken houses, or brethren, or sisters, of father, or mother, or wife, or children, or lands, for my name's sake, shall receive an hundredfold, and shall inherit everlasting life.

MATTHEW 19:29

Thy testimonies have I taken as an heritage for ever: for they are the rejoicing of my heart.

PSALM 119:111

For evildoers shall be cut off: but those that wait upon the LORD, they shall inherit the earth. . . .

The meek shall inherit the earth; and shall delight themselves in the abundance of peace.

PSALM 37:9, 11

Riches and honour are with me: yea, durable riches and righteousness.

My fruit is better than gold, yea, than fine gold; and my revenue than choice silver.

I lead in the way of righteousness, in the midst of the paths of judgment:

That I may cause those that love me to inherit substance; and I will fill their treasures.

PROVERBS 8:18–21

Not rendering evil for evil, or railing for railing: but contrariwise blessing; knowing that ye are thereunto called, that ye should inherit a blessing.

1 PETER 3:9

Lord God,
Thank You for my heritage.
I pray for the members of my family,
that they will live a life pleasing to You
and will continue the Christian heritage.
May they consider my life to have been
one of faithful service to You.
Amen.

Homemaking

Grandparents' homes are gathering places for the extended family. They are places of memories and warmth and love, secure shelters for children and grandchildren alike. What a wonderful gift we give when we open our houses to our loved ones. Remember, almost all of Christ's ministry, including the Last Supper, took place in people's homes. He wants our homes today to still be places of ministry and blessing.

And there ye shall eat before the LORD your God, and ye shall rejoice in all that ye put your hand unto, ye and your households, wherein the LORD thy God hath blessed thee.

DEUTERONOMY 12:7

And they said, Believe on the Lord Jesus Christ, and thou shalt be saved, and thy house.

ACTS 16:31

*Y*our home should reflect the personalities, passions, and priorities of those who live there.

TERRY WILLITS

The curse of the LORD is in the house of the wicked: but he blesseth the habitation of the just.

PROVERBS 3:33

But as for me and my house, we will serve the LORD.

JOSHUA 24:15

The wicked are overthrown, and are not: but the house of the righteous shall stand.

PROVERBS 12:7

Through wisdom is an house builded; and by understanding it is established.

PROVERBS 24:3

Except the LORD build the house, they labour in vain that build it.

PSALM 127:1

And my people shall dwell in a peaceable habitation, and in sure dwellings, and in quiet resting places.

ISAIAH 32:18

Our holy and our beautiful house, where our fathers praised thee. . .

ISAIAH 64:11

Wisdom hath builded her house.

PROVERBS 9:1

Better is a dry morsel, and quietness therewith, than an house full of sacrifices with strife.

PROVERBS 17:1

Peace be to this house.

LUKE 10:5

Moses was faithful in all his house. . . .
For every house is builded by some man; but he that built all things is God.

HEBREWS 3:2, 4

Lord Jesus,
I dedicate my home to You.
Fill it with joy and love.
Thank You for the beautiful memories
our family has created in my home.
May it continue to be a haven for those most special to me.
Amen.

Hope

Sometimes we feel as though we have nothing left to hope for. When we feel like that, though, we are deceived by the devil. The hope God gives us is more than a cheery and optimistic outlook on life. Instead, it is a confidence founded on God's faithfulness, and it will only grow stronger with the years.

I wait for the LORD, my soul doth wait, and in his word do I hope.

PSALM 130:5

The hope of the righteous shall be gladness: but the expectation of the wicked shall perish.

PROVERBS 10:28

But sanctify the Lord God in your hearts: and be ready always to give an answer to every man that asketh you a reason of the hope that is in you with meekness and fear.

1 PETER 3:15

*O*ptimism is the faith that
leads to achievement.
Nothing can be done without
hope and confidence.
HELEN KELLER

Why art thou cast down, O my soul? and why art thou disquieted in me? hope thou in God: for I shall yet praise him for the help of his countenance.

PSALM 42:5

Beloved, now are we the sons of God, and it doth not yet appear what we shall be: but we know that, when he shall appear, we shall be like him; for we shall see him as he is.

And every man that hath this hope in him purifieth himself, even as he is pure.

1 JOHN 3:2–3

But let us, who are of the day, be sober, putting on the breastplate of faith and love; and for an helmet, the hope of salvation.

1 THESSALONIANS 5:8

The wicked is driven away in his wickedness: but the righteous hath hope in his death.

PROVERBS 14:32

We glory in tribulations also: knowing that tribulation worketh patience;

And patience, experience; and experience, hope:

And hope maketh not ashamed; because the love of God is shed abroad in our hearts by the Holy Ghost which is given unto us.

ROMANS 5:3–5

My soul fainteth for thy salvation: but I hope in thy word. . . .

Thou art my hiding place and my shield: I hope in thy word.

PSALM 119:81, 114

The LORD is my portion, saith my soul; therefore will I hope in him.

The LORD is good unto them that wait for him, to the soul that seeketh him.

It is good that a man should both hope and quietly wait for the salvation of the LORD.

LAMENTATIONS 3:24–26

Blessed is the man that trusteth in the LORD, and whose hope the LORD is.

JEREMIAH 17:7

Now the God of hope fill you with all joy and peace in believing, that ye may abound in hope, through the power of the Holy Ghost.

ROMANS 15:13

Blessed be the God and Father of our Lord Jesus Christ, which according to his abundant mercy hath begotten us again unto a lively hope by the resurrection of Jesus Christ from the dead.

1 PETER 1:3

But I will hope continually, and will yet praise thee more and more.

PSALM 71:14

Father,

Thank You for the hope I have in You.
At times I can use the word casually.
I may say, "I hope it doesn't rain today,"
or "I hope to complete my errands."
But these pale in significance when
I think of Your hope—
a deep, strong, everlasting hope.
Amen.

Hospitality

God calls us to give what we have—and this means opening our homes, both to our loved ones and to strangers, that we might share the wealth of love with which our homes have been blessed. Not only does our hospitality minister to our family and friends, but it also ministers to Christ Himself.

But whoso hath this world's good, and seeth his brother have need, and shutteth up his bowels of compassion from him, how dwelleth the love of God in him?

1 JOHN 3:17

Let brotherly love continue.

Be not forgetful to entertain strangers: for thereby some have entertained angels unawares.

HEBREWS 13:1–2

*H*appy is the house that
shelters a friend.

RALPH WALDO EMERSON

Let love be without dissimulation. Abhor that which is evil; cleave to that which is good. . . .

Distributing to the necessity of saints; given to hospitality.

ROMANS 12:9, 13

For a bishop must be blameless, as the steward of God; not selfwilled, not soon angry. . .not given to filthy lucre;

But a lover of hospitality.

TITUS 1:7–8

Charity shall cover the multitude of sins.

Use hospitality one to another without grudging.

1 PETER 4:8–9

Lord, when saw we thee an hungred, and fed thee? or thirsty, and gave thee drink?

When saw we thee a stranger, and took thee in? or naked, and clothed thee? . . .

And the King shall answer. . .Inasmuch as ye have done it unto one of the least of these my brethren, ye have done it unto me.

MATTHEW 25:37–38, 40

A certain woman named Martha received him into her house.

And she had a sister called Mary, which also sat at Jesus' feet, and heard his word.

But Martha was cumbered about much serving, and came to him, and said, Lord, dost thou not care that my sister hath left me to serve alone? bid her therefore that she help me.

And Jesus answered and said unto her, Martha, Martha, thou art careful and troubled about many things:

But one thing is needful: and Mary hath chosen that good part, which shall not be taken away from her.

LUKE 10:38–42

Lord Jesus,
I want my home to be a place where others feel welcome.
May I create a warm, inviting environment for others.
Please don't let me be overcome with preparations.
May my visitors feel at home here,
and make this place one where You are
happy to reside, too, Lord.
Amen.

Joy

Our lives are rich with joys: new grandchildren to love and hold, our pride in our family's achievements, a lifetime of love to look back and reflect on. God has truly blessed us!

Hitherto have ye asked nothing in my name: ask, and ye shall receive, that your joy may be full.

JOHN 16:24

For our heart shall rejoice in him, because we have trusted in his holy name.

PSALM 33:21

My soul shall be satisfied as with marrow and fatness; and my mouth shall praise thee with joyful lips.

PSALM 63:5

*H*ow much better it is to weep at joy
than to joy at weeping.

WILLIAM SHAKESPEARE

I will greatly rejoice in the LORD, my soul shall be joyful in my God; for he hath clothed me with the garments of salvation, he hath covered me with the robe of righteousness, as a bridegroom decketh himself with ornaments, and as a bride adorneth herself with her jewels.

ISAIAH 61:10

Go your way, eat the fat, and drink the sweet, and send portions unto them for whom nothing is prepared: for this day is holy unto our LORD: neither be ye sorry; for the joy of the LORD is your strength.

NEHEMIAH 8:10

But let the righteous be glad; let them rejoice before God: yea, let them exceedingly rejoice.

Sing unto God, sing praises to his name: extol him that rideth upon the heavens by his name JAH, and rejoice before him.

PSALM 68:3–4

The righteous shall be glad in the LORD, and shall trust in him; and all the upright in heart shall glory.

PSALM 64:10

The voice of rejoicing and salvation is in the tabernacles of the righteous: the right hand of the LORD doeth valiantly.

PSALM 118:15

Light is sown for the righteous, and gladness for the upright in heart.

PSALM 97:11

For ye shall go out with joy, and be led forth with peace: the mountains and the hills shall break forth before you into singing, and all the trees of the field shall clap their hands.

ISAIAH 55:12

Thou hast put gladness in my heart, more than in the time that their corn and their wine increased.

PSALM 4:7

Thou wilt shew me the path of life: in thy presence is fulness of joy; at thy right hand there are pleasures for evermore.

PSALM 16:11

Rejoice in the Lord alway: and again I say, Rejoice.

PHILIPPIANS 4:4

A merry heart doeth good like a medicine: but a broken spirit drieth the bones.

PROVERBS 17:22

Therefore the redeemed of the LORD shall return, and come with singing unto Zion; and everlasting joy shall be upon their head: they shall obtain gladness and joy; and sorrow and mourning shall flee away.

ISAIAH 51:11

Rejoice ye in that day, and leap for joy: for, behold, your reward is great in heaven: for in the like manner did their fathers unto the prophets.

LUKE 6:23

God,
We have a tendency to rush through life.
The here and now tend to supersede all other thoughts.
Help me to remember that horizons exist that
we can neither see nor comprehend. . .
eternal joy, eternal hope.
It's all ours if we are Yours.
Amen.

Justice

Our lives should be examples to our children and grandchildren, models that they can look to for patterns of living. Because others are watching us, we can't afford to allow any room in our lives for injustice and dishonesty. How important it is, then, that our own model be the life of our Lord. Again and again, the Bible tells us that only by faith can we live just lives. When we walk in the light of our faith, then our families will see in us examples of justice and truth.

Finally, brethren, whatsoever things are true, whatsoever things are honest, whatsoever things are just. . .if there be any virtue, and if there be any praise, think on these things.

PHILIPPIANS 4:8

*N*ever look for righteousness
in the other person,
but never cease to be righteous yourself.
We are always looking for justice,
yet the essence of the teaching of
the Sermon on the Mount is—
Never look for justice,
but never cease to give it.

OSWALD CHAMBERS

For I am not ashamed of the gospel of Christ: for it is the power of God unto salvation to every one that believeth. . . .

For therein is the righteousness of God revealed from faith to faith: as it is written, The just shall live by faith.

ROMANS 1:16–17

Who is wise, and he shall understand these things? prudent, and he shall know them? for the ways of the LORD are right, and the just shall walk in them.

HOSEA 14:9

There shall no evil happen to the just: but the wicked shall be filled with mischief.

PROVERBS 12:21

A good man leaveth an inheritance to his children's children: and the wealth of the sinner is laid up for the just.

PROVERBS 13:22

The wicked is snared by the transgression of his lips: but the just shall come out of trouble.

PROVERBS 12:13

But that no man is justified by the law in the sight of God, it is evident: for, The just shall live by faith.

GALATIANS 3:11

The just man walketh in his integrity: his children are blessed after him.

PROVERBS 20:7

Now the just shall live by faith: but if any man draw back, my soul shall have no pleasure in him.

HEBREWS 10:38

Behold, his soul which is lifted up is not upright in him: but the just shall live by his faith.

HABAKKUK 2:4

Dear God,
Make me a just and honest person in all areas of my life.
Help me to be consistent so that others will
want to act justly, too.
Amen.

Learning

Sometimes we may be tempted to think we have learned all that there is to learn. After all, the years have taught us many lessons. The Bible reminds us, though, about the kind of learning that is truly important. No matter how old we are, we will always have more to learn about the Lord.

A wise man will hear, and will increase learning; and a man of understanding shall attain unto wise counsels:

To understand a proverb, and the interpretation; the words of the wise, and their dark sayings.

PROVERBS 1:5–6

It is good for me that I have been afflicted; that I might learn thy statutes.

PSALM 119:71

*L*earning is not attained by chance;
it must be sought for with ardor
and attended to with diligence.

ABIGAIL ADAMS

And it shall be with him, and he shall read therein all the days of his life: that he may learn to fear the LORD his God, to keep all the words of this law and these statutes, to do them.

DEUTERONOMY 17:19

Learn to do well; seek judgment, relieve the oppressed, judge the fatherless, plead for the widow.

ISAIAH 1:17

Good and upright is the LORD: therefore will he teach sinners in the way.

The meek will he guide in judgment: and the meek will he teach his way.

PSALM 25:8–9

Take my yoke upon you, and learn of me; for I am meek and lowly in heart: and ye shall find rest unto your souls.

MATTHEW 11:29

The Lord GOD. . .wakeneth morning by morning, he wakeneth mine ear to hear as the learned.

ISAIAH 50:4

But continue thou in the things which thou hast learned and hast been assured of, knowing of whom thou hast learned them;

And that from a child thou hast known the holy scriptures, which are able to make thee wise unto salvation through faith which is in Christ Jesus.

2 TIMOTHY 3:14–15

They also that erred in spirit shall come to understanding, and they that murmured shall learn doctrine.

ISAIAH 29:24

Blessed art thou, O LORD: teach me thy statutes. . . .

I have declared my ways, and thou heardest me: teach me thy statutes.

PSALM 119:12, 26

And when they bring you unto the synagogues, and unto magistrates, and powers, take ye no thought how or what thing ye shall answer, or what ye shall say:

For the Holy Ghost shall teach you in the same hour what ye ought to say.

LUKE 12:11–12

Now therefore go, and I will be with thy mouth, and teach thee what thou shalt say.

EXODUS 4:12

Teach me, and I will hold my tongue: and cause me to understand wherein I have erred.

JOB 6:24

Though the Lord give you the bread of adversity, and the water of affliction, yet shall not thy teachers be removed into a corner any more, but thine eyes shall see thy teachers:

And thine ears shall hear a word behind thee, saying, This is the way, walk ye in it, when ye turn to the right hand, and when ye turn to the left.

ISAIAH 30:20–21

Teach me to do thy will; for thou art my God: thy spirit is good; lead me into the land of uprightness.

PSALM 143:10

I will instruct thee and teach thee in the way which thou shalt go: I will guide thee with mine eye.

PSALM 32:8

Accept, I beseech thee, the freewill offerings of my mouth,
O LORD, and teach me thy judgments.

PSALM 119:108

Heavenly Father,
I have gained much knowledge and experience over the years.
Please let me be willing to share with others
what You have taught me.
Help me to never be content with what I've learned,
but continue to seek knowledge.
Amen.

Long Life

*A*s grandparents, God has given us a long life filled with His blessings.

Ye shall walk in all the ways which the LORD your God hath commanded you, that ye may live, and that it may be well with you, and that ye may prolong your days in the land which ye shall possess.

DEUTERONOMY 5:33

*D*o not worry;

eat three square meals a day;

say your prayers;

be courteous to your creditors;

keep your digestion good;

exercise; go slow and easy.

Maybe there are other things your special case

requires to make you happy;

but, my friend,

these I reckon will give you a good life.

ABRAHAM LINCOLN

For by me thy days shall be multiplied, and the years of thy life shall be increased.

PROVERBS 9:11

That thou mightest fear the LORD thy God, to keep all his statutes and his commandments, which I command thee, thou, and thy son, and thy son's son, all the days of thy life; and that thy days may be prolonged.

DEUTERONOMY 6:2

Thou shalt come to thy grave in a full age, like as a shock of corn cometh in in his season.

JOB 5:26

What man is he that desireth life, and loveth many days, that he may see good?

Keep thy tongue from evil, and thy lips from speaking guile.

Depart from evil, and do good; seek peace, and pursue it.

PSALM 34:12–14

That thou mayest love the LORD thy God, and that thou mayest obey his voice, and that thou mayest cleave unto him: for he is thy life, and the length of thy days.

DEUTERONOMY 30:20

He that dwelleth in the secret place of the most High shall abide under the shadow of the Almighty. . . .

He shall call upon me, and I will answer him: I will be with him in trouble; I will deliver him, and honour him.

With long life will I satisfy him, and shew him my salvation.

PSALM 91:1, 15–16

The fear of the LORD prolongeth days: but the years of the wicked shall be shortened.

PROVERBS 10:27

The righteous shall flourish like the palm tree: he shall grow like a cedar in Lebanon.

Those that be planted in the house of the LORD shall flourish in the courts of our God.

They shall still bring forth fruit in old age; they shall be fat and flourishing.

PSALM 92:12–14

My son, forget not my law; but let thine heart keep my commandments:

For length of days, and long life, and peace, shall they add to thee.

PROVERBS 3:1–2

Even to your old age I am he; and even to hoar hairs will I carry you: I have made, and I will bear; even I will carry, and will deliver you.

ISAIAH 46:4

Happy is the man that findeth wisdom, and the man that getteth understanding. . . .

Length of days is in her right hand; and in her left hand riches and honour.

PROVERBS 3:13, 16

Lord,
Even though I might want to deny it,
I realize that my mirror tells the truth.
As I look at my changing features,
may I be reminded of Your changeless love
and pray that You might be reflected in
every smile, every word, and every breath.
Amen.

Love

Love is a two-way street: The more we give, the more we will get back. The more love we show to our children and grandchildren, to our neighbors, to all with whom we come into contact, and to God our heavenly Father, the more He will shower His love on us.

Hear, O Israel: The LORD our God is one LORD:

And thou shalt love the LORD thy God with all thine heart, and with all thy soul, and with all thy might.

DEUTERONOMY 6:4–5

But whoso keepeth his word, in him verily is the love of God perfected: hereby know we that we are in him. . . .

He that loveth his brother abideth in the light, and there is none occasion of stumbling in him.

1 JOHN 2:5, 10

*T*hey do not love that
do not show their love.

WILLIAM SHAKESPEARE

But as it is written, Eye hath not seen, nor ear heard, neither have entered into the heart of man, the things which God hath prepared for them that love him.

1 CORINTHIANS 2:9

I love them that love me; and those that seek me early shall find me.

PROVERBS 8:17

He that hath my commandments, and keepeth them, he it is that loveth me: and he that loveth me shall be loved of my Father, and I will love him, and will manifest myself to him.

JOHN 14:21

But as touching brotherly love ye need not that I write unto you: for ye yourselves are taught of God to love one another.

1 THESSALONIANS 4:9

A new commandment I give unto you, That ye love one another; as I have loved you, that ye also love one another.

By this shall all men know that ye are my disciples, if ye have love one to another.

JOHN 13:34–35

Seeing ye have purified your souls in obeying the truth through the Spirit unto unfeigned love of the brethren, see that ye love one another with a pure heart fervently.

1 PETER 1:22

Let love be without dissimulation. Abhor that which is evil; cleave to that which is good.

Be kindly affectioned one to another with brotherly love; in honour preferring one another.

ROMANS 12:9–10

Though I have the gift of prophecy, and understand all mysteries, and all knowledge; and though I have all faith, so that I could remove mountains, and have not charity, I am nothing. . . .

Charity suffereth long, and is kind; charity envieth not; charity vaunteth not itself, is not puffed up.

Doth not behave itself unseemly, seeketh not her own, is not easily provoked, thinketh no evil;

Rejoiceth not in iniquity, but rejoiceth in the truth;

Beareth all things, believeth all things, hopeth all things, endureth all things.

Charity never faileth. . . .

And now abideth faith, hope, charity, these three; but the greatest of these is charity.

1 CORINTHIANS 13:2, 4–8, 13

The Lord preserveth all them that love him: but all the wicked will he destroy.

PSALM 145:20

Grace be with all them that love our Lord Jesus Christ in sincerity.

EPHESIANS 6:24

My little children, let us not love in word, neither in tongue; but in deed and in truth.

1 JOHN 3:18

Keep yourselves in the love of God.

JUDE 21

Put on therefore, as the elect of God, holy and beloved, bowels of mercies, kindness, humbleness of mind, meekness, longsuffering;

Forbearing one another, and forgiving one another. . . .

And above all these things put on charity, which is the bond of perfectness.

COLOSSIANS 3:12–14

Beloved, let us love one another: for love is of God; and every one that loveth is born of God, and knoweth God. . . . He that loveth not knoweth not God; for God is love.

Herein is love, not that we loved God, but that he loved us, and sent his Son to be the propitiation for our sins.

Beloved, if God so loved us, we ought also to love one another.

1 JOHN 4:7, 10–11

Dear God,
Thank You for loving me.
May I share that same love
unconditionally with others.
Amen.

Mercy

We have a lifetime of joys to look back on—but we also have a lifetime of sin and mistakes. Our God, though, is a merciful God; He forgives our sins and remembers them no more. Why should we continue to trouble ourselves with what God has forgotten? Instead, we can rest in His mercy.

And therefore will the LORD wait, that he may be gracious unto you, and therefore will he be exalted, that he may have mercy upon you: for the LORD is a God of judgment: blessed are all they that wait for him.

ISAIAH 30:18

*T*each me to feel another's woe,
To hide the fault I see;
That mercy I to others show,
That mercy show to me.

ALEXANDER POPE

And the publican, standing afar off, would not lift up so much as his eyes unto heaven, but smote upon his breast, saying, God be merciful to me a sinner.

I tell you, this man went down to his house justified rather than the other: for every one that exalteth himself shall be abased; and he that humbleth himself shall be exalted.

LUKE 18:13–14

Blessed are the merciful: for they shall obtain mercy.

MATTHEW 5:7

And they shall not teach every man his neighbour, and every man his brother, saying, Know the Lord: for all shall know me, from the least to the greatest.

For I will be merciful to their unrighteousness, and their sins and their iniquities will I remember no more.

HEBREWS 8:11–12

And the LORD passed by before him, and proclaimed, The LORD, The LORD God, merciful and gracious, longsuffering, and abundant in goodness and truth.

Keeping mercy for thousands, forgiving iniquity and transgression and sin.

EXODUS 34:6–7

And rend your heart, and not your garments, and turn unto the LORD your God: for he is gracious and merciful, slow to anger, and of great kindness, and repenteth him of the evil.

JOEL 2:13

Many sorrows shall be to the wicked: but he that trusteth in the LORD, mercy shall compass him about.

PSALM 32:10

Wherefore in all things it behoved him to be made like unto his brethren, that he might be a merciful and faithful high priest in things pertaining to God, to make reconciliation for the sins of the people.

HEBREWS 2:17

It is of the LORD's mercies that we are not consumed, because his compassions fail not.

They are new every morning: great is thy faithfulness.

LAMENTATIONS 3:22–23

Mercy and truth are met together; righteousness and peace have kissed each other.

Truth shall spring out of the earth; and righteousness shall look down from heaven.

PSALM 85:10–11

The LORD is merciful and gracious, slow to anger, and plenteous in mercy.

PSALM 103:8

*B*ehold, the eye of the LORD is
upon them that fear him,
upon them that hope in his mercy.

PSALM 33:18

And his mercy is on them that fear him from generation to generation.

LUKE 1:50

And Mary said, . . .

And his mercy is on them that fear him from generation to generation. . . .

And her neighbours and her cousins heard how the Lord had shewed great mercy upon [Elisabeth]; and they rejoiced with her.

LUKE 1:46, 50, 58

Let thy tender mercies come unto me, that I may live: for thy law is my delight. . . .

Great are thy tender mercies, O LORD: quicken me according to thy judgments.

PSALM 119:77, 156

Be ye therefore merciful, as your Father also is merciful.

LUKE 6:36

For thou, Lord, art good, and ready to forgive; and plenteous in mercy unto all them that call upon thee.

PSALM 86:5

Blessed be the God and Father of our Lord Jesus Christ, which according to his abundant mercy hath begotten us again unto a lively hope by the resurrection of Jesus Christ from the dead.

1 PETER 1:3

The LORD is good to all: and his tender mercies are over all his works.

PSALM 145:9

Father,
At times I find myself keeping a mental tally of
wrongs others have committed against me.
Forgive me!
You have forgotten all of my sins and failures.
Please help me to erase my "memory chalkboard"
and show mercy to others.
Amen.

Parental Example

*O*ne of our most important jobs as grandparents is to show our faith by the example of our lives to our children and grandchildren.

When I call to remembrance the unfeigned faith that is in thee, which dwelt first in thy grandmother Lois, and thy mother Eunice; and I am persuaded that in thee also.

2 TIMOTHY 1:5

Observe and hear all these words which I command thee, that it may go well with thee, and with thy children after thee for ever, when thou doest that which is good and right in the sight of the LORD thy God.

DEUTERONOMY 12:28

*L*ove begins at home,
and it is not how much we do. . .
but how much love we put in that action.

MOTHER TERESA

And these words, which I command thee this day, shall be in thine heart:
And thou shalt teach them diligently unto thy children.

DEUTERONOMY 6:6–7

Tell ye your children of it, and let your children tell their children, and their children another generation.

JOEL 1:3

Blessed is every one that feareth the LORD; that walketh in his ways. . . .

The LORD shall bless thee out of Zion: and thou shalt see the good of Jerusalem all the days of thy life.

Yea, thou shalt see thy children's children, and peace upon Israel.

PSALM 128:1, 5–6

Therefore shall ye lay up these my words in your heart and in your soul. . . .

And ye shall teach them your children, speaking of them when thou sittest in thine house.

DEUTERONOMY 11:18–19

When your children shall ask their fathers in time to come. . .

Then ye shall let your children know. . .

That all the people of the earth might know the hand of the LORD, that it is mighty: they ye might fear the LORD your God for ever.

JOSHUA 4:21–22, 24

Train up a child in the way he should go: and when he is old, he will not depart from it.

PROVERBS 22:6

For I know him, that he will command his children and his household after him, and they shall keep the way of the LORD, to do justice and judgment.

GENESIS 18:19

Dear Lord,
Thank You for giving me the strength and wisdom I
needed as I raised my child.
I pray for this family
as they now train my grandchild in You.
Please help them—and me—
to be examples of You, the perfect, loving Father.
Amen.

Patience

*O*ur grandchildren are not apt to be patient—they want what they want now. In our lives, we can demonstrate to them the importance and beauty of patience.

That ye be not slothful, but followers of them who through faith and patience inherit the promises.

HEBREWS 6:12

Rest in the LORD, and wait patiently for him: fret not thyself because of him who prospereth in his way, because of the man who bringeth wicked devices to pass.

PSALM 37:7

I choose patience. . . .

I will overlook the inconveniences of the world.

Instead of cursing the one who takes my place,

I'll invite him to do so.

Rather than complain that the wait is too long,

I will thank God for a moment to pray.

MAX LUCADO

Because thou hast kept the word of my patience, I also will keep thee from the hour of temptation, which shall come upon all the world, to try them that dwell upon the earth.

REVELATION 3:10

And the servant of the Lord must not strive; but be gentle unto all men, apt to teach, patient,

In meekness instructing those that oppose themselves; if God peradventure will give them repentance to the acknowledging of the truth.

2 TIMOTHY 2:24–25

Better is the end of a thing than the beginning thereof: and the patient in spirit is better than the proud in spirit.

ECCLESIASTES 7:8

Cast not away therefore your confidence, which hath great recompense of reward.

For ye have need of patience, that, after ye have done the will of God, ye might receive the promise.

HEBREWS 10:35–36

And not only so, but we glory in tribulations also: knowing that tribulation worketh patience;

And patience, experience; and experience, hope:

And hope maketh not ashamed; because the love of God is shed abroad in our hearts by the Holy Ghost which is given unto us.

ROMANS 5:3–5

For whatsoever things were written aforetime were written for our learning, that we through patience and comfort of the scriptures might have hope.

ROMANS 15:4

And so, after he [Abraham] had patiently endured, he obtained the promise.

HEBREWS 6:15

We are bound to thank God always for you, brethren, as it is meet, because that your faith groweth exceedingly, and the charity of every one of you all toward each other aboundeth;

So that we ourselves glory in you in the churches of God for your patience and faith in all your persecutions and tribulations that ye endure.

2 THESSALONIANS 1:3–4

Wherefore seeing we also are compassed about with so great a cloud of witnesses, let us lay aside every weight, and the sin which doth so easily beset us, and let us run with patience the race that is set before us.

HEBREWS 12:1

I waited patiently for the LORD; and he inclined unto me, and heard my cry.

PSALM 40:1

Knowing this, that the trying of your faith worketh patience.

But let patience have her perfect work, that ye may be perfect and entire, wanting nothing.

JAMES 1:3–4

In your patience possess ye your souls.

LUKE 21:19

God,
Let me grow in the area of patience.
Help me to remember that when You make
a squash, it takes four weeks;
but when You make a strong oak,
it takes a hundred years.
Let me be patient knowing that You're working miracles
in my life as You "grow me" into Your likeness.
Amen.

Peace

Peace is God's gift to us. It's a gift we can possess in the midst of sorrow and sickness, just as much as in joy and health; for in human terms, it is a peace "which passeth understanding" (Philippians 4:7).

Great peace have they which love thy law: and nothing shall offend them.

PSALM 119:165

For the mountains shall depart, and the hills be removed; but my kindness shall not depart from thee, neither shall the covenant of my peace be removed, saith the LORD that hath mercy on thee.

ISAIAH 54:10

*C*hrist alone can bring lasting peace—
peace with God—
peace among men and nations—
and peace within our hearts.

BILLY GRAHAM

Now the God of hope fill you with all joy and peace in believing, that ye may abound in hope, through the power of the Holy Ghost.

ROMANS 15:13

And all thy children shall be taught of the LORD; and great shall be the peace of thy children.

ISAIAH 54:13

For ye shall go out with joy, and be led forth with peace: the mountains and the hills shall break forth before you into singing, and all the trees of the field shall clap their hands.

ISAIAH 55:12

The LORD will give strength unto his people; the LORD will bless his people with peace.

PSALM 29:11

Peace I leave with you, my peace I give unto you: not as the world giveth, give I unto you. Let not your heart be troubled, neither let it be afraid.

JOHN 14:27

Therefore being justified by faith, we have peace with God through our Lord Jesus Christ.

ROMANS 5:1

But the meek shall inherit the earth; and shall delight themselves in the abundance of peace.

PSALM 37:11

Mark the perfect man, and behold the upright: for the end of that man is peace.

PSALM 37:37

When a man's ways please the LORD, he maketh even his enemies to be at peace with him.

PROVERBS 16:7

Thou wilt keep him in perfect peace, whose mind is stayed on thee: because he trusteth in thee.

ISAIAH 26:3

And the very God of peace sanctify you wholly; and I pray God your whole spirit and soul and body be preserved blameless unto the coming of our Lord Jesus Christ.

1 THESSALONIANS 5:23

For he that will love life, and see good days, let him refrain his tongue from evil, and his lips that they speak no guile:
    Let him eschew evil, and do good; let him seek peace, and ensue it.

1 PETER 3:10–11

These things I have spoken unto you, that in me ye might have peace. In the world ye shall have tribulation: but be of good cheer; I have overcome the world.

JOHN 16:33

I will both lay me down in peace, and sleep: for thou, LORD, only makest me dwell in safety.

PSALM 4:8

Blessed are the peacemakers: for they shall be called the children of God.

MATTHEW 5:9

And the peace of God, which passeth all understanding, shall keep your hearts and minds through Christ Jesus.

PHILIPPIANS 4:7

Praise the LORD, O Jerusalem; praise thy God, O Zion.

For he hath strengthened the bars of thy gates; he hath blessed thy children within thee.

He maketh peace in thy borders, and filleth thee with the finest of the wheat.

PSALM 147:12–14

Follow peace with all men, and holiness, without which no man shall see the Lord.

HEBREWS 12:14

Lord,
There is so much activity and so many distractions in life.
Please calm my spirit,
and help me to rest in Your perfect peace.
Amen.

Prayer

*P*rayer is the way we communicate with God. It is the pipeline that connects us with Him and allows His blessings to flow to us. As grandparents, many of us are called to a special ministry of prayer for our families and loved ones.

But thou, when thou prayest, enter into thy closet, and when thou hast shut thy door, pray to thy Father which is in secret; and thy Father which seeth in secret shall reward thee openly.

MATTHEW 6:6

For then shalt thou have thy delight in the Almighty, and shalt lift up thy face unto God.

Thou shalt make thy prayer unto him, and he shall hear thee, and thou shalt pay thy vows.

JOB 22:26–27

*P*rayer is in very deed
the pulse of the spiritual life.
It is the great means of bringing to minister
and people the blessing and power of heaven.
Persevering and believing prayer means
a strong and an abundant life.

ANDREW MURRAY

He shall call upon me, and I will answer him.

PSALM 91:15

Be careful for nothing; but in every thing by prayer and supplication with thanksgiving let your requests be made known unto God.

And the peace of God, which passeth all understanding, shall keep your hearts and minds through Christ Jesus.

PHILIPPIANS 4:6–7

The effectual fervent prayer of a righteous man availeth much.

Elias. . .prayed earnestly that it might not rain: and it rained not on the earth by the space of three years and six months.

And he prayed again, and the heaven gave rain, and the earth brought forth her fruit.

JAMES 5:16–18

Whatsoever ye shall ask the Father in my name, he will give it you.

Hitherto have ye asked nothing in my name: ask, and ye shall receive, that your joy may be full.

JOHN 16:23–24

Lord, teach us to pray, as John also taught his disciples.

And he said unto them, When ye pray, say, Our Father which art in heaven, Hallowed be thy name. Thy kingdom come. Thy will be done, as in heaven, so in earth.

Give us day by day our daily bread.

And forgive us our sins; for we also forgive every one that is indebted to us. And lead us not into temptation; but deliver us from evil. . . .

And I say unto you, Ask, and it shall be given you; seek, and ye shall find; knock, and it shall be opened unto you. . . .

If a son shall ask bread of any of you that is a father, will he give him a stone? or if he ask a fish, will he for a fish give him a serpent? . . .

If ye then, being evil, know how to give good gifts unto your children: how much more shall your heavenly Father give the Holy Spirit to them that ask him?

LUKE 11:1–4, 9, 11, 13

And it shall come to pass, that before they call, I will answer; and while they are yet speaking, I will hear.

ISAIAH 65:24

Then shall ye call upon me, and ye shall go and pray unto me, and I will hearken unto you.

And ye shall seek me, and find me, when ye shall search for me with all your heart.

JEREMIAH 29:12–13

And this is the confidence that we have in him, that, if we ask any thing according to his will, he heareth us:

And if we know that he hear us, whatsoever we ask, we know that we have the petitions that we desired of him.

1 JOHN 5:14–15

Call unto me, and I will answer thee, and shew thee great and mighty things, which thou knowest not.

JEREMIAH 33:3

Evening, and morning, and at noon, will I pray, and cry aloud: and he shall hear my voice.

PSALM 55:17

Men ought always to pray, and not to faint.

LUKE 18:1

He will be very gracious unto thee at the voice of thy cry; when he shall hear it, he will answer thee.

ISAIAH 30:19

The LORD is nigh unto all them that call upon him, to all that call upon him in truth.

PSALM 145:18

Ask, and it shall be given you; seek, and ye shall find; knock, and it shall be opened unto you:

For every one that asketh receiveth; and he that seeketh findeth; and to him that knocketh it shall be opened.

MATTHEW 7:7–8

Again I say unto you, That if two of you shall agree on earth as touching any thing that they shall ask, it shall be done for them of my Father which is in heaven.

For where two or three are gathered together in my name, there am I in the midst of them.

MATTHEW 18:19–20

*I*f my people,
which are called by my name,
shall humble themselves,
and pray, and seek my face,
and turn from their wicked ways;
then will I hear from heaven,
and will forgive their sin,
and will heal their land.

2 CHRONICLES 7:14

Likewise the Spirit also helpeth our infirmities: for we know not what we should pray for as we ought: but the Spirit itself maketh intercession for us with groanings which cannot be uttered.

ROMANS 8:26

Let us therefore come boldly unto the throne of grace, that we may obtain mercy, and find grace to help in time of need.

HEBREWS 4:16

Dear God,
I pray for my family.
At times I want to help when they are hurting,
but may I be reminded that the most effective thing
I can do is pray for them.
Thank You for listening to me when I come to You,
and teach me to be quiet and listen for Your response.
Amen.

Prosperity

God promises prosperity to those who love Him. We may not be rich in the world's eyes, but nevertheless, these are years when we should allow ourselves to enjoy the many riches God has bestowed on us.

Every man also to whom God hath given riches and wealth, and hath given him power to eat thereof, and to take his portion, and to rejoice in his labour; this is the gift of God.

ECCLESIASTES 5:19

And also that every man should eat and drink, and enjoy the good of all his labour, it is the gift of God.

ECCLESIASTES 3:13

*I*f we had no winter
the spring would not be so pleasant;
if we did not sometimes taste of adversity,
prosperity would not be so welcome.

ANNE BRADSTREET

This book of the law shall not depart out of thy mouth; but thou shalt meditate therein day and night, that thou mayest observe to do according to all that is written therein: for then thou shalt make thy way prosperous, and then thou shalt have good success.

JOSHUA 1:8

The LORD shall make thee plenteous in goods. . . .

The LORD shall open unto thee his good treasure. . .to bless all the work of thine hand. . . .

If that thou hearken unto the commandments of the LORD thy GOD.

DEUTERONOMY 28:11–13

In the house of the righteous is much treasure: but in the revenues of the wicked is trouble.

PROVERBS 15:6

In the day of prosperity be joyful.

ECCLESIASTES 7:14

Then shall he give the rain of thy seed, that thou shalt sow the ground withal; and bread of the increase of the earth, and it shall be fat and plenteous: in that day shall thy cattle feed in large pastures.

ISAIAH 30:23

I wisdom dwell with prudence. . . .

Riches and honour are with me; yea, durable riches and righteousness.

My fruit is better than gold, yea, than fine gold; and my revenue than choice silver.

I lead in the way of righteousness, in the midst of the paths of judgment:

That I may cause those that love me to inherit substance; and I will fill their treasures.

PROVERBS 8:12, 18–21

But lay up for yourselves treasures in heaven. . . .

For where your treasure is, there will your heart be also.

MATTHEW 6:20–21

Blessed is the man that feareth the LORD, that delighteth greatly in his commandments.

His seed shall be mighty upon earth: the generation of the upright shall be blessed.

Wealth and riches shall be in his house: and his righteousness endureth for ever.

PSALM 112:1–3

Let the LORD be magnified, which hath pleasure in the prosperity of his servant.

PSALM 35:27

If thou shalt hearken diligently unto the voice of the LORD thy God, to observe and to do all his commandments which I command thee this day. . .

All these blessings shall come on thee, and overtake thee. . . .

Blessed shalt thou be in the city, and blessed shalt thou be in the field. . . .

Blessed shall be thy basket and thy store.

Blessed shalt thou be when thou comest in, and blessed shalt thou be when thou goest out.

DEUTERONOMY 28:1–3, 5–6

And in every work that he began. . .to seek his God, he [Hezekiah] did it with all his heart, and prospered.

2 CHRONICLES 31:21

Thank You,
Lord, for Your many riches in my life.
Financially I may not be wealthy,
but I have my family and friends,
and they are much more important
to me than monetary affluence.
I praise You for Your provision.
Amen.

Protection

$\mathcal{S}$ometimes when we listen to the nightly news or read the newspapers, the many stories about crime and violence may frighten us. We live in a world that's often unsafe—and yet we need not be afraid. Our God has promised to "preserve thee from all evil: he shall preserve thy soul" (Psalm 121:7). Despite the world's dangers, we can rest in the protection of God's love.

The eternal God is thy refuge, and underneath are the everlasting arms: and he shall thrust out the enemy from before thee; and shall say, Destroy them.

DEUTERONOMY 33:27

*H*e will silently plan for thee,

Object thought or omniscient care;

God Himself undertakes to be

Thy Pilot through each subtle snare.

E. MARY GRIMES

Shew thy marvellous lovingkindness, O thou that savest by thy right hand them which put their trust in thee from those that rise up against them.

Keep me as the apple of the eye, hide me under the shadow of thy wings,

From the wicked that oppress me, from my deadly enemies, who compass me about.

PSALM 17:7–9

I am with thee, and will keep thee in all places whither thou goest.

GENESIS 28:15

Thou art my hiding place; thou shalt preserve me from trouble; thou shalt compass me about with songs of deliverance.

PSALM 32:7

Thus saith the LORD, In an acceptable time have I heard thee, and in a day of salvation have I helped thee: and I will preserve thee.

ISAIAH 49:8

For I said in my haste, I am cut off from before thine eyes: nevertheless thou heardest the voice of my supplications when I cried unto thee.

O love the LORD, all ye his saints: for the Lord preserveth the faithful.

PSALM 31:22–23

Be not afraid of sudden fear, neither of the desolation of the wicked, when it cometh.

For the LORD shall be thy confidence, and shall keep thy foot from being taken.

PROVERBS 3:25–26

My help cometh from the LORD, which made heaven and earth.

He will not suffer thy foot to be moved: he that keepeth thee will not slumber. . . .

The LORD shall preserve thy going out and thy coming in from this time forth, and even for evermore.

PSALM 121:2–3, 8

But mine eyes are unto thee, O God the Lord: in thee is my trust; leave not my soul destitute.

Keep me from the snares which they have laid for me, and the gins of the workers of iniquity.

Let the wicked fall into their own nets, whilst that I withal escape.

PSALM 141:8–10

Hold thou me up, and I shall be safe.

PSALM 119:117

Behold, the eye of the LORD is upon them that fear him, upon them that hope in his mercy;

To deliver their soul from death, and to keep them alive in famine.

PSALM 33:18–19

For the LORD our God, he it is that brought us up and our fathers out of the land of Egypt, from the house of bondage, and which did those great signs in our sight, and preserved us in all the way wherein we went, and among all the people through whom we passed.

JOSHUA 24:17

The Lord is nigh unto all them that call upon him, to all that call upon him in truth.

He will fulfil the desire of them that fear him: he also will hear their cry, and will save them.

The LORD preserveth all them that love him.

PSALM 145:18–20

Then shalt thou walk in thy way safely, and thy foot shall not stumble.

When thou liest down, thou shalt not be afraid: yea, thou shalt lie down, and thy sleep shall be sweet.

Be not afraid of sudden fear, neither of the desolation of the wicked, when it cometh.

For the LORD shall be thy confidence, and shall keep thy foot from being taken.

PROVERBS 3:23–26

For the oppression of the poor, for the sighing of the needy, now will I arise, saith the LORD; I will set him in safety from him that puffeth at him.

PSALM 12:5

In the fear of the LORD
is strong confidence:
and his children shall have
a place of refuge.

PROVERBS 14:26

The fear of man bringeth a snare: but whoso putteth his trust in the LORD shall be safe.

PROVERBS 29:25

Above all, taking the shield of faith, wherewith ye shall be able to quench all the fiery darts of the wicked.

EPHESIANS 6:16

And he said, The LORD is my rock, and my fortress, and my deliverer;

The God of my rock; in him will I trust: he is my shield, and the horn of my salvation, my high tower, and my refuge, my saviour; thou savest me from violence.

I will call on the LORD, who is worthy to be praised: so shall I be saved from mine enemies.

2 SAMUEL 22:2–4

God is our refuge and strength, a very present help in trouble.

Therefore will not we fear, though the earth be removed, and though the mountains be carried into the midst of the sea;

Though the waters thereof roar and be troubled, though the mountains shake with the swelling thereof.

PSALM 46:1–3

When thou passest through the waters, I will be with thee; and through the rivers, they shall not overflow thee: when thou walkest through the fire, thou shalt not be burned; neither shall the flame kindle upon thee.

ISAIAH 43:2

Lord,
I may not realize the "close calls" I've had,
but I thank You for Your hand of protection on me.
I don't want to be consumed with the threat of danger,
for You have promised to always be with me.
Thank You for keeping me safe in Your care.
Amen.

Repentance

*N*o matter how old we are, we never outgrow our need for repentance. Just as our human relationships are damaged when we refuse to say we're sorry, so our relationship with God will not flourish if we fail to examine our hearts and apologize to Him for the ways we have failed. What's more, repentance carries with it the promise of change. They say you can't teach an old dog new tricks—but true repentance is a gift of grace, and thanks to Christ's salvation at work in our hearts, we are never too old to change.

The Lord is not slack concerning his promise, as some men count slackness; but is longsuffering to us-ward, not willing that any should perish, but that all should come to repentance.

2 PETER 3:9

The goodness of God leadeth to repentance.

ROMANS 2:4

*R*epentance is a change of willing,
of feeling and of living,
in respect to God.

CHARLES FINNEY

Have mercy upon me, O God, according to thy lovingkindness: according unto the multitude of thy tender mercies blot out my transgressions.

Wash me thoroughly from mine iniquity, and cleanse me from my sin.

For I acknowledge my transgressions: and my sin is ever before me.

PSALM 51:1–3

Except ye repent, ye shall all likewise perish.

LUKE 13:3

Now I rejoice, not that ye were made sorry, but that ye sorrowed to repentance: for ye were made sorry after a godly manner. . . .

For godly sorrow worketh repentance to salvation. . .but the sorrow of the world worketh death.

2 CORINTHIANS 7:9–10

The LORD is nigh unto them that are of a broken heart; and saveth such as be of a contrite spirit.

PSALM 34:18

If iniquity be in thine hand, put it far away, and let not wickedness dwell in thy tabernacles.

For then shalt thou lift up thy face without spot; yea, thou shalt be steadfast, and shalt not fear.

JOB 11:14–15

I say unto you, that likewise joy shall be in heaven over one sinner that repenteth, more than over ninety and nine just persons, which need no repentance. . . .

I say unto you, there is joy in the presence of the angels of God over one sinner that repenteth.

LUKE 15:7, 10

Because he considereth, and turneth away from all his transgressions that he hath committed, he shall surely live, he shall not die. . . .

Repent, and turn yourselves from all your transgressions; so iniquity shall not be your ruin.

EZEKIEL 18:28, 30

Therefore say unto the house of Israel, Thus saith the Lord GOD; Repent, and turn yourselves from your idols; and turn away your faces from all your abominations.

EZEKIEL 14:6

Repent ye therefore, and be converted, that your sins may be blotted out, when the times of refreshing shall come from the presence of the Lord.

ACTS 3:19

Draw nigh to God, and he will draw nigh to you. Cleanse your hands, ye sinners; and purify your hearts, ye double minded.

JAMES 4:8

As many as I love, I rebuke and chasten: be zealous therefore, and repent.

Behold, I stand at the door, and knock: if any man hear my voice, and open the door, I will come in to him, and will sup with him, and he with me.

To him that overcometh will I grant to sit with me in my throne, even as I also overcame, and am set down with my Father in his throne.

REVELATION 3:19–21

He that covereth his sins shall not prosper: but whoso confesseth and forsaketh them shall have mercy.

PROVERBS 28:13

Lord Jesus,
I repent of the sins I commit against You.
Help me not to be too proud to acknowledge
when I wrong You or others.
Change my heart, so that I leave these sins in the past.
Amen.

Rest

 L ife seems so tiring sometimes. When our minds and bodies and hearts are weary, though, we need to remember to turn to our heavenly Father, for He has promised to give us rest.

There remaineth therefore a rest to the people of God.

For he that is entered into his rest, he also hath ceased from his own works, as God did from his.

Let us labour therefore to enter into that rest.

HEBREWS 4:9–11

*E*very now and then, go away,
have a little relaxation,
for when you come back to your work
your judgment will be surer.
Go some distance away because
then the work appears smaller,
and more of it can be taken in at a glance
and a lack of harmony and
proportion is more readily seen.

LEONARDO DA VINCI

For ye are not as yet come to the rest and to the inheritance, which the LORD your God giveth you.

DEUTERONOMY 12:9

He maketh the storm a calm, so that the waves thereof are still.

Then are they glad because they be quiet; so he bringeth them unto their desired haven.

PSALM 107:29–30

Return unto thy rest, O my soul; for the LORD hath dealt bountifully with thee.

PSALM 116:7

Come unto me, all ye that labour and are heavy laden, and I will give you rest.

Take my yoke upon you, and learn of me; for I am meek and lowly in heart: and ye shall find rest unto your souls.

For my yoke is easy, and my burden is light.

MATTHEW 11:28–30

LORD, my heart is not haughty, nor mine eyes lofty: neither do I exercise myself in great matters, or in things too high for me.

Surely I have behaved and quieted myself, as a child that is weaned of his mother: my soul is even as a weaned child.

PSALM 131:1–2

And the work of righteousness shall be peace; and the effect of righteousness quietness and assurance for ever.

And my people shall dwell in a peaceable habitation, and in sure dwellings, and in quiet resting places.

ISAIAH 32:17–18

For now should I have lain still and been quiet, I should have slept: then had I been at rest. . . .

There the wicked cease from troubling; and there the weary be at rest.

JOB 3:13, 17

He maketh me to lie down in green pastures: he leadeth me beside the still waters.

PSALM 23:2

Rest in the LORD, and wait patiently for him.

PSALM 37:7

I will both lay me down in peace, and sleep: for thou, LORD, only makest me dwell in safety.

PSALM 4:8

When thou liest down, thou shalt not be afraid: yea, thou shalt lie down, and thy sleep shall be sweet.

PROVERBS 3:24

He that dwelleth in the secret place of the most High shall abide under the shadow of the Almighty.

PSALM 91:1

Dear Lord,
I will rest in You today.
Please rejuvenate my body so that I can
accomplish great things for You.
Amen.

Scripture

A s a grandparent, many will come to you seeking your wise counsel. Be prepared by reading and studying the scriptures. God's Word will enlighten your heart and your mind.

And that from a child thou hast known the holy scriptures, which are able to make thee wise unto salvation through faith which is in Christ Jesus.

2 TIMOTHY 3:15

*I*t is comforting that this Book
has indeed manifested a peculiar ability
to speak to the deepest needs and
communicated the gospel effectively to
people of all different times, places, and customs.
The obstacle of culture cannot
make void the power of this Word.

R. C. SPROUL

Therefore shall ye lay up these my words in your heart and in your soul, and bind them for a sign upon your hand, that they may be as frontlets between your eyes.

And ye shall teach them your children, speaking of them when thou sittest in thine house, and when thou walkest by the way, when thou liest down, and when thou risest up.

DEUTERONOMY 11:18–19

That ye may be mindful of the words which were spoken before by the holy prophets, and of the commandment of us the apostles of the Lord and Saviour.

2 PETER 3:2

Thy word have I hid in mine heart, that I might not sin against thee.

PSALM 119:11

For the word of God is quick, and powerful, and sharper than any twoedged sword, piercing even to the dividing asunder of soul and spirit, and of the joints and marrow, and is a discerner of the thoughts and intents of the heart.

HEBREWS 4:12

So shall my word be that goeth forth out of my mouth: it shall not return unto me void, but it shall accomplish that which I please, and it shall prosper in the thing whereto I sent it.

ISAIAH 55:11

This book of the law shall not depart out of thy mouth; but thou shalt meditate therein day and night, that thou mayest observe to do according to all that is written therein: for then thou shalt make thy way prosperous, and then thou shalt have good success.

JOSHUA 1:8

Thy word is a lamp unto my feet, and a light unto my path.

PSALM 119:105

Seek ye out of the book of the LORD, and read: no one of these shall fail, none shall want her mate: for my mouth it hath commanded, and his spirit it hath gathered them.

ISAIAH 34:16

Thank You,
God, for giving us Your Word.
Let me emphasize its importance to my grandchildren,
so that they can hide Your words in their hearts.
May they see the true joy that results from
the time spent reading Your truth.
Amen.

Seeking God

What's the secret to a full and happy life? As the scriptures say, those who "seek the LORD shall not want any good thing" (Psalm 34:10). Continually seek Him in Your life, and enjoy the abundance of blessings He bestows upon you.

But seek ye first the kingdom of God, and his righteousness; and all these things shall be added unto you.

MATTHEW 6:33

Sow to yourselves in righteousness, reap in mercy; break up your fallow ground: for it is time to seek the LORD, till he come and rain righteousness upon you.

HOSEA 10:12

*W*e need never shout
across the spaces to an absent God.
He is nearer than our own soul,
closer than our most secret thoughts.

A. W. TOZER

With my soul have I desired thee in the night; yea, with my spirit within me will I seek thee early: for when thy judgments are in the earth, the inhabitants of the world will learn righteousness.

ISAIAH 26:9

Seek the LORD and his strength, seek his face continually.

1 CHRONICLES 16:11

Seek the LORD, and ye shall live.

AMOS 5:6

And ye shall seek me, and find me, when ye shall search for me with all your heart.

JEREMIAH 29:13

One thing have I desired of the LORD, that will I seek after; that I may dwell in the house of the LORD all the days of my life, to behold the beauty of the LORD, and to enquire in his temple.

PSALM 27:4

Therefore came I forth to meet thee, diligently to seek thy face, and I have found thee.

PROVERBS 7:15

But if from thence thou shalt seek the LORD thy God, thou shalt find him, if thou seek him with all thy heart and with all thy soul.

DEUTERONOMY 4:29

Glory ye in his holy name: let the heart of them rejoice that seek the LORD.

1 CHRONICLES 16:10

But rather seek ye the kingdom of God; and all these things shall be added unto you.

LUKE 12:31

Let the heart of them rejoice that seek the LORD.
  Seek the LORD, and his strength; seek his face evemore.
PSALM 105:3–4

Heavenly Father,
I want to know You better every day.
Please don't let me be content with having a steady,
familiar relationship with You.
Just as relationships with friends and family
only deepen by spending time together,
so does my relationship with You.
Amen.

Self-Denial

Sometimes we think God is asking us to give up too much: our career, our health, our home, sometimes even loved ones. It just doesn't seem fair. Denying ourselves does not come easily to any of us, no matter our age. And yet each loss that time brings us can be looked at as a chance to deny ourselves, so that Christ may live in place of our selfish natures.

If any man will come after me, let him deny himself, and take up his cross, and follow me.

For whosoever will save his life shall lose it: and whosoever will lose his life for my sake shall find it.

MATTHEW 16:24–25

*T*o deny ourselves is
to simply say no to our desires
when they conflict with God's will.

CHARLES STANLEY

Therefore, brethren, we are debtors, not to the flesh, to live after the flesh.

For if ye live after the flesh, ye shall die: but if ye through the Spirit do mortify the deeds of the body, ye shall live.

ROMANS 8:12–13

Verily I say unto you, There is no man that hath left house, or parents, or brethren, or wife, or children, for the kingdom of God's sake,

Who shall not receive manifold more in this present time, and in the world to come life everlasting.

LUKE 18:29–30

For the grace of God that bringeth salvation hath appeared to all men. . . .

Looking for that blessed hope, and the glorious appearing of the great God and our Saviour Jesus Christ.

TITUS 2:11, 13

But I say unto you, That ye resist not evil: but whosoever shall smite thee on thy right cheek, turn to him the other also.

And if any man will sue thee at the law, and take away thy coat, let him have thy cloak also.

And whosoever shall compel thee to go a mile, go with him twain.

Give to him that asketh thee, and from him that would borrow of thee turn not thou away.

MATTHEW 5:39–42

And they that are Christ's have crucified the flesh with the affections and lusts.

If we live in the Spirit, let us also walk in the Spirit.

GALATIANS 5:24–25

Lord,
Take away my selfishness.
I commit every area of my life to You
for Your will to be done.
Amen

Separation

*A*s we get older, it seems that more and more often we are separated from those we love so much. Our children take jobs on the other side of the country, and as a result, we miss the delight of watching our grandchildren grow and develop. Old friends move away. And with increasing frequency death touches our lives with the ultimate separation. How comforting, though, to know that no matter where our loved ones are, they are still in God's hands!

The LORD watch between me and thee, when we are absent one from another.

GENESIS 31:49

*R*ecognize that everyone feels. . .
lonely for a while.
Allow it to happen,
and accept yourself where you are.

GARY BENNETT

For I am persuaded, that neither death, nor life. . .nor things present, nor things to come,

Nor height, nor depth, nor any other creature, shall be able to separate us from the love of God, which is in Christ Jesus our Lord.

ROMANS 8:38–39

As cold waters to a thirsty soul, so is good news from a far country.

PROVERBS 25:25

Lo, I am with you alway, even unto the end of the world.

MATTHEW 28:20

But we, brethren, being taken from you for a short time in presence, not in heart, endeavoured the more abundantly to see your face with great desire.

1 Thessalonians 2:17

The Lord bless thee, and keep thee:

The Lord make his face shine upon thee, and be gracious unto thee:

The Lord lift up his countenance upon thee, and give thee peace.

Numbers 6:24–26

Pray. . .that I may be restored to you the sooner.

Hebrews 13:18–19

Dear God,
It's hard for me to be separated from
those who are so very special to me.
I commit them to Your care.
Thank You that although we may experience
separation on earth,
You have prepared a place for us
to all be together with You forever.
Amen.

Sickness

*B*eing sick is difficult. But even in sickness, God is with us in a special way.

Lord, behold, he whom thou lovest is sick.

JOHN 11:3

Himself took our infirmities, and bare our sicknesses.

MATTHEW 8:17

*S*ickness, thou mayest intrude;
but I have a balsam ready—
God has chosen me.
Whatever befall me in this vale of tears,
I know that He has chosen me.

CHARLES SPURGEON

My grace is sufficient for thee: for my strength is made perfect in weakness. Most gladly therefore will I rather glory in my infirmities, that the power of Christ may rest upon me.

2 CORINTHIANS 12:9

Have mercy upon me, O LORD; for I am weak: O LORD, heal me.

PSALM 6:2

He giveth power to the faint; and to them that have no might he increaseth strength.

ISAIAH 40:29

My flesh and my heart faileth: but God is the strength of my heart, and my portion for ever.

PSALM 73:26

Yea, though I walk through the valley of the shadow of death, I will fear no evil: for thou art with me.

PSALM 23:4

And Jesus went about. . .healing all manner of sickness and all manner of disease among the people.

MATTHEW 4:23

And ye shall serve the LORD your God, and he shall bless thy bread, and thy water; and I will take sickness away from the midst of thee.

EXODUS 23:25

Hath God forgotten to be gracious? hath he in anger shut up his tender mercies?

And I said, This is my infirmity: but I will remember the years of the right hand of the most High.

I will remember the works of the LORD: surely I will remember thy wonders of old.

I will meditate also of all thy work, and talk of thy doings.

PSALM 77:9–12

And the LORD will take away from thee all sickness.

DEUTERONOMY 7:15

A bruised reed shall he not break.

MATTHEW 12:20

Dear Father,
I want to be thankful "in [the midst of] all things."
Experiencing illness is difficult,
so I pray for the grace and the strength I need for today.
Amen.

Sorrow

Times of sorrow and loss come to all our lives. Jesus Himself was called "a man of sorrows, and acquainted with grief" (Isaiah 53:3). He understands what we feel, and even in our grief He is with us. As the hymnist wrote, "When sorrows like sea billows roll," we can still say, "it is well with my soul."

Save me, O God; for the waters are come in unto my soul.

PSALM 69:1

When thou passest through the waters, I will be with thee; and through the rivers, they shall not overflow thee.

ISAIAH 43:2

A single sunbeam is
enough to drive away many shadows.

ST. FRANCIS OF ASSISI

Surely he hath borne our griefs, and carried our sorrows.

ISAIAH 53:4

O my Father, if it be possible, let this cup pass from me: nevertheless not as I will, but as thou wilt.

MATTHEW 26:39

He hath sent me to bind up the brokenhearted.

ISAIAH 61:1

The eternal God is thy refuge, and underneath are the everlasting arms.

DEUTERONOMY 33:27

They that sow in tears shall reap in joy.

He that goeth forth and weepeth, bearing precious seed, shall doubtless come again with rejoicing, bringing his sheaves with him.

PSALM 126:5–6

The Lord said, I have surely seen the affliction of my people. . .for I know their sorrows.

And I am come down to deliver them.

EXODUS 3:7–8

In all their affliction he was afflicted, and the angel of his presence saved them: in his love and in his pity he redeemed them; and he bare them, and carried them all the days of old.

ISAIAH 63:9

Then when Mary was come where Jesus was, and saw him, she fell down at his feet, saying unto him, Lord, if thou hadst been here, my brother had not died.

When Jesus therefore saw her weeping, and the Jews also weeping which came with her, he groaned in the spirit, and was troubled,

And said, Where have ye laid him? They said unto him, Lord, come and see.

Jesus wept.

JOHN 11:32–35

Sorrow and sighing shall flee away.

ISAIAH 35:10

Your sorrow shall be turned into joy.

JOHN 16:20

Dear God,
Thank You for being my companion
in the midst of my sorrow.
At times the grief seems unbearable,
but You will be my comfort.
I'm reassured by the fact that You have experienced grief,
so You know just what I need.
Carry me through this difficult time, I pray.
Amen.

Strength

*O*ur physical strength may not be as great as it was when we were younger. But God gives to us another type of strength, and the Bible promises that our youth will be "renewed like the eagle's" (Psalm 103:5).

[Abraham] staggered not at the promise of God through unbelief; but was strong in faith, giving glory to God;

And being fully persuaded that, what he had promised, he was able also to perform.

ROMANS 4:20–21

Then I said, I have laboured in vain, I have spent my strength for nought, and in vain: yet surely my judgment is with the LORD, and my work with my God.

And now, saith the LORD that formed me from the womb to be his servant, to bring Jacob again to him, Though Israel be not gathered, yet shall I be glorious in the eyes of the LORD, and my God shall be my strength.

ISAIAH 49:4–5

*W*e must continue to ask God for wisdom
and insight and for the strength to persevere.
He will cause us to rise up and fly like eagles,
walking and not fainting.

NORMA SMALLEY

When I am weak, then am I strong.

2 CORINTHIANS 12:10

Behold, God is my salvation; I will trust, and not be afraid: for the LORD JEHOVAH is my strength and my song; he also is become my salvation.

ISAIAH 12:2

For every one that useth milk is unskilful in the word of righteousness: for he is a babe.

But strong meat belongeth to them that are of full age, even those who by reason of use have their senses exercised to discern both good and evil.

HEBREWS 5:13–14

They that wait upon the LORD shall renew their strength; they shall mount up with wings as eagles; they shall run, and not be weary; and they shall walk, and not faint.

ISAIAH 40:31

The joy of the LORD is your strength.

NEHEMIAH 8:10

Let him take hold of my strength, that he may make peace with me; and he shall make peace with me.

ISAIAH 27:5

In returning and rest shall ye be saved; in quietness and in confidence shall be your strength.

ISAIAH 30:15

Seek the Lord and his strength, seek his face continually.

1 CHRONICLES 16:11

The Lord is my strength and song, and he is become my salvation.

EXODUS 15:2

I will love thee, O LORD, my strength.

The LORD is my rock, and my fortress, and my deliverer; my God, my strength, in whom I will trust; my buckler, and the horn of my salvation, and my high tower.

PSALM 18:1–2

Thy God hath commanded thy strength: strengthen, O God, that which thou hast wrought for us.

PSALM 68:28

Through faith also Sara herself received strength to conceive seed, and was delivered of a child when she was past age, because she judged him faithful who had promised.

HEBREWS 11:11

O man greatly beloved, fear not:
peace be unto thee,
be strong, yea, be strong.

DANIEL 10:19

For thou art my hope, O Lord GOD: thou art my trust from my youth.

By thee have I been holden up from the womb: thou art he that took me out of my mother's bowels: my praise shall be continually of thee.

I am as a wonder unto many; but thou art my strong refuge.

Let my mouth be filled with thy praise and with thy honour all the day.

Cast me not off in the time of old age; forsake me not when my strength faileth.

PSALM 71:5–8

Wait on the LORD: be of good courage, and he shall strengthen thine heart: wait, I say, on the LORD.

PSALM 27:14

The LORD will give strength unto his people; the LORD will bless his people with peace.

PSALM 29:11

My flesh and my heart faileth: but God is the strength of my heart, and my portion for ever.

PSALM 73:26

And he said unto me, My grace is sufficient for thee: for my strength is made perfect in weakness. Most gladly therefore will I rather glory in my infirmities, that the power of Christ may rest upon me.

2 CORINTHIANS 12:9

I can do all things through Christ which strengtheneth me.

PHILIPPIANS 4:13

He giveth power to the faint; and to them that have no might he increaseth strength.

ISAIAH 40:29

Lord,
As I feel the effects of the years,
I pray for the strength to forge ahead.
I ask today not only for physical strength,
but also for spiritual strength.
Amen.

Thanksgiving

We have so much in our lives for which to be thankful. Let us not forget to offer up our thanksgiving to God.

As ye have therefore received Christ Jesus the Lord, so walk ye in him:

Rooted and built up in him, and stablished in the faith, as ye have been taught, abounding therein with thanksgiving.

COLOSSIANS 2:6–7

Continue in prayer, and watch in the same with thanksgiving.

COLOSSIANS 4:2

*G*ratitude is
the heart's money.
FRENCH PROVERB

Oh that men would praise the LORD for his goodness, and for his wonderful works to the children of men!

And let them sacrifice the sacrifices of thanksgiving, and declare his works with rejoicing.

PSALM 107:21–22

Be careful for nothing; but in every thing by prayer and supplication with thanksgiving let your requests be made known unto God.

PHILIPPIANS 4:6

Blessing, and glory, and wisdom, and thanksgiving, and honour, and power, and might, be unto our God for ever and ever. Amen.

REVELATION 7:12

Make a joyful noise unto the LORD, all ye lands.

Serve the LORD with gladness: come before his presence with singing.

Know ye that the Lord he is God: it is he that hath made us, and not we ourselves; we are his people, and the sheep of his pasture.

Enter into his gates with thanksgiving, and into his courts with praise: be thankful unto him, and bless his name.

For the LORD is good; his mercy is everlasting; and his truth endureth to all generations.

PSALM 100

I will praise thee, O LORD, with my whole heart; I will shew forth all thy marvellous works.

I will be glad and rejoice in thee: I will sing praise to thy name, O thou most High.

PSALM 9:1–2

Blessed be the LORD, that hath given rest unto his people Israel, according to all that he promised: there hath not failed one word of all his good promise, which he promised by the hand of Moses his servant.

1 KINGS 8:56

For all things are for your sakes, that the abundant grace might through the thanksgiving of many redound to the glory of God.

For which cause we faint not; but though our outward man perish, yet the inward man is renewed day by day.

For our light affliction, which is but for a moment, worketh for us a far more exceeding and eternal weight of glory.

2 CORINTHIANS 4:15–17

Being enriched in every thing to all bountifulness, which causeth through us thanksgiving to God.

For the administration of this service not only supplieth the want of the saints, but is abundant also by many thanksgivings unto God.

2 CORINTHIANS 9:11–12

O LORD, thou hast brought up my soul from the grave: thou hast kept me alive, that I should not go down to the pit.

PSALM 30:3

Giving thanks always for all things unto God and the Father in the name of our Lord Jesus Christ.

EPHESIANS 5:20

In every thing give thanks: for this is the will of God in Christ Jesus concerning you.

1 THESSALONIANS 5:18

Many, O LORD my God, are thy wonderful works which thou hast done, and thy thoughts which are to us-ward: they cannot be reckoned up in order unto thee: if I would declare and speak of them, they are more than can be numbered.

PSALM 40:5

Thou hast turned for me my mourning into dancing: thou hast put off my sackcloth, and girded me with gladness;

To the end that my glory may sing praise to thee, and not be silent. O LORD my God, I will give thanks unto thee for ever.

PSALM 30:11–12

He that regardeth the day, regardeth it unto the Lord; and he that regardeth not the day, to the Lord he doth not regard it. He that eateth, eateth to the Lord, for he giveth God thanks; and he that eateth not, to the Lord he eateth not, and giveth God thanks.

ROMANS 14:6

I will praise the name of God with a song, and will magnify him with thanksgiving.

PSALM 69:30

It is a good thing to give thanks unto the LORD, and to sing praises unto thy name, O most High:

To shew forth thy lovingkindness in the morning, and thy faithfulness every night.

PSALM 92:1–2

Sing unto the LORD with thanksgiving; sing praise upon the harp unto our God.

PSALM 147:7

O give thanks unto the LORD; for he is good: for his mercy endureth for ever.

PSALM 136:1

I will mention the lovingkindnesses of the LORD, and the praises of the LORD, according to all that the LORD hath bestowed on us, and the great goodness toward the house of Israel, which he hath bestowed on them according to his mercies, and according to the multitude of his lovingkindnesses.

ISAIAH 63:7

*B*lessed be the Lord,
who daily loadeth us with benefits,
even the God of our salvation.

PSALM 68:19

Offer unto God thanksgiving; and pay thy vows unto the most High.

PSALM 50:14

Thank You,
Heavenly Father,
for all You've done and all You are in my life.
I thank You for my family, too,
and for the memories we have together.
I want to always have a thankful spirit.
Amen.

Trouble

*T*roubles of one sort or another come to everyone. Financial worries, health problems, concern for our families, loss, and grief—none of these are too big for our God to handle.

O my Father, if it be possible, let this cup pass from me: nevertheless not as I will, but as thou wilt.

MATTHEW 26:39

We have not an high priest which cannot be touched with the feeling of our infirmities; but was in all points tempted like as we are, yet without sin.

Let us therefore come boldly unto the throne of grace, that we may. . .find grace to help in time of need.

HEBREWS 4:15–16

*E*xpect trouble as an inevitable part of life,
and repeat to yourself
the most comforting words of all:
"This, too, shall pass."
ANN LANDERS

He shall call upon me, and I will answer him: I will be with him in trouble.

PSALM 91:15

Be not far from me; for trouble is near.

PSALM 22:11

Casting all your care upon him; for he careth for you.

1 PETER 5:7

My heart is sore pained within me: and the terrors of death are fallen upon me.

Fearfulness and trembling are come upon me, and horror hath overwhelmed me.

And I said, Oh that I had wings like a dove! for then would I fly away, and be at rest.

PSALM 55:4–6

I cried unto the LORD with my voice; with my voice unto the LORD did I make my supplication.

I poured out my complaint before him; I shewed before him my trouble.

When my spirit was overwhelmed within me, then thou knewest my path. In the way wherein I walked have they privily laid a snare for me.

I looked on my right hand, and beheld, but there was no man that would know me: refuge failed me; no man cared for my soul.

I cried unto thee, O LORD: I said, Thou art my refuge and my portion in the land of the living.

Attend unto my cry; for I am brought very low: deliver me from my persecutors; for they are stronger than I.

Bring my soul out of prison, that I may praise thy name: the righteous shall compass me about; for thou shalt deal bountifully with me.

PSALM 142

His compassions fail not. . . .

For he doth not afflict willingly nor grieve the children of men.

LAMENTATIONS 3:22, 33

Who shall separate us from the love of Christ? shall tribulation, or distress. . . ?

Nay, in all these things we are more than conquerors through him that loved us.

ROMANS 8:35, 37

Beloved, think it not strange concerning the fiery trial which is to try you, as though some strange thing happened unto you.

But rejoice, inasmuch as ye are partakers of Christ's sufferings.

1 PETER 4:12–13

*W*hen my heart is overwhelmed:
lead me to the rock that is higher than I.

PSALM 61:2

He that toucheth you toucheth the apple of [God's] eye.

ZECHARIAH 2:8

Now our Lord Jesus Christ himself, and God, even our Father, which hath loved us, and hath given us everlasting consolation and good hope through grace,

Comfort your hearts.

2 THESSALONIANS 2:16–17

The Father of mercies, and the God of all comfort;

Who comforteth us in all our tribulation, that we may be able to comfort them which are in any trouble, by the comfort wherewith we ourselves are comforted of God.

2 CORINTHIANS 1:3–4

My times are in thy hand: deliver me from the hand of mine enemies, and from them that persecute me.

PSALM 31:15

For the mountains shall depart, and the hills be removed; but my kindness shall not depart from thee, neither shall the covenant of my peace be removed, saith the LORD that hath mercy on thee.

O thou afflicted, tossed with tempest, and not comforted, behold, I will lay thy stones with fair colours, and lay thy foundations with sapphires.

ISAIAH 54:10–11

Dear God,
I'm facing a difficulty again.
Remind me that You are bigger than anything
I have to confront in life.
Help me to learn from this hardship,
so that I can encourage others who
may also experience this adversity.
Amen.

Trust

When troubles overtake us, the only way we can grab hold of God's peace is through trust.

Thou wilt keep him in perfect peace, whose mind is stayed on thee: because he trusteth in thee.

Trust ye in the LORD for ever: for in the LORD JEHOVAH is everlasting strength.

ISAIAH 26:3–4

Be merciful unto me, O God, be merciful unto me: for my soul trusteth in thee: yea, in the shadow of thy wings will I make my refuge, until these calamities be overpast.

PSALM 57:1

*S*ometimes we are to guard our heart. . .

protect it from invasion and keep things safe

and secure. Sometimes we should give our heart. . .

let certain qualities out and release them to others.

CHARLES SWINDOLL

It is better to trust in the LORD than to put confidence in man.

It is better to trust in the LORD than to put confidence in princes.

PSALM 118:8–9

Many sorrows shall be to the wicked: but he that trusteth in the LORD, mercy shall compass him about.

PSALM 32:10

They that trust in the LORD shall be as mount Zion, which cannot be removed, but abideth for ever.

PSALM 125:1

But we had the sentence of death in ourselves, that we should not trust in ourselves, but in God which raiseth the dead:

Who delivered us from so great a death, and doth deliver: in whom we trust that he will yet deliver us.

2 CORINTHIANS 1:9–10

The God of my rock; in him will I trust: he is my shield, and the horn of my salvation, my high tower, and my refuge, my saviour; thou savest me from violence.

2 SAMUEL 22:3

I will say of the LORD, He is my refuge and my fortress: my God; in him will I trust. . . .

He shall cover thee with his feathers, and under his wings shalt thou trust.

PSALM 91:2, 4

He shall not be afraid of evil tidings: his heart is fixed, trusting in the LORD.

His heart is established, he shall not be afraid.

PSALM 112:7–8

Trust in the LORD with all thine heart; and lean not unto thine own understanding.

In all thy ways acknowledge him, and he shall direct thy paths.

PROVERBS 3:5–6

Lord Jesus,
I put my complete trust in You.
I rely solely on You.
Amen.

Vigilance

*E*ven when our bodies are at rest, no longer as active as they once may have been, our hearts and minds are still active, and we must be vigilant, alert, and watchful that sin finds no room in our souls.

Be sober, be vigilant; because your adversary the devil, as a roaring lion, walketh about, seeking whom he may devour:

Whom resist stedfast in the faith, knowing that the same afflictions are accomplished in your brethren that are in the world.

1 PETER 5:8–9

*T*he devil is not terribly frightened of
our human efforts and credentials.
But he knows his kingdom will be damaged
when we begin to lift up our hearts to God.

JIM CYMBALA

My heart is fixed, O God, my heart is fixed: I will sing and give praise.

Awake up, my glory; awake, psaltery and harp: I myself will awake early.

PSALM 57:7–8

But watch thou in all things, endure afflictions, do the work of an evangelist, make full proof of thy ministry.

2 TIMOTHY 4:5

And he cometh unto the disciples, and findeth them asleep, and saith unto Peter, What, could ye not watch with me one hour?

Watch and pray, that ye enter not into temptation: the spirit indeed is willing, but the flesh is weak.

MATTHEW 26:40–41

But ye, brethren, are not in darkness, that that day should overtake you as a thief.

Ye are all the children of light, and the children of the day: we are not of the night, nor of darkness.

Therefore let us not sleep, as do others; but let us watch and be sober.

1 THESSALONIANS 5:4–6

And that, knowing the time, that now it is high time to awake out of sleep: for now is our salvation nearer than when we believed.

The night is far spent, the day is at hand: let us therefore cast off the works of darkness, and let us put on the armour of light.

ROMANS 13:11–12

My soul waiteth for the Lord more than they that watch for the morning: I say, more than they that watch for the morning.

PSALM 130:6

Wherefore he saith, Awake thou that sleepest, and arise from the dead, and Christ shall give thee light.

EPHESIANS 5:14

Behold, I come as a thief. Blessed is he that watcheth, and keepeth his garments, lest he walk naked, and they see his shame.

REVELATION 16:15

Watch ye, stand fast in the faith, quit you like men, be strong.

1 CORINTHIANS 16:13

Lord,
Keep me alert,
so that I may avoid anything that would displease You.
Protect me from Satan's attempts to make me falter.
For "greater is he that is in [me],
than he that is in the world" (1 John 4:4).
Amen.

Wisdom

Through the years, the Lord has taught us much. This wisdom is a precious gift, one that we can humbly share with our families, always remembering that we can take no credit for our wisdom, for it is a gift from the Lord.

The law of the LORD is perfect, converting the soul: the testimony of the LORD is sure, making wise the simple.

PSALM 19:7

Wisdom strengtheneth the wise more than ten mighty men which are in the city.

ECCLESIASTES 7:19

*A*ge brings experience,
and a good mind wisdom.
GREEK PROVERB

The fruit of the righteous is a tree of life; and he that winneth souls is wise.

PROVERBS 11:30

Happy is the man that findeth wisdom, and the man that getteth understanding.

PROVERBS 3:13

Whoso is wise, and will observe these things, even they shall understand the lovingkindness of the LORD.

PSALM 107:43

Then shall the kingdom of heaven be likened unto ten virgins. . . .

And five of them were wise, and five were foolish.

They that were foolish took their lamps, and took no oil with them:

But the wise took oil in their vessels with their lamps. . . .

While [the foolish] went to buy, the bridegroom came; and they that were ready went in with him to the marriage: and the door was shut.

MATTHEW 25:1–4, 10

And they that be wise shall shine as the brightness of the firmament; and they that turn many to righteousness as the stars for ever and ever.

DANIEL 12:3

But the wisdom that is from above is first pure, then peaceable, gentle, and easy to be intreated, full of mercy and good fruits, without partiality, and without hypocrisy.

JAMES 3:17

Therefore whosoever heareth these sayings of mine, and doeth them, I will liken him unto a wise man, which built his house upon a rock:

And the rain descended, and the floods came, and the winds blew, and beat upon that house; and it fell not: for it was founded upon a rock.

MATTHEW 7:24–25

He that handleth a matter wisely shall find good: and whoso trusteth in the LORD, happy is he.

The wise in heart shall be called prudent: and the sweetness of the lips increaseth learning.

PROVERBS 16:20–21

How much better is it to get wisdom than gold! and to get understanding rather to be chosen than silver!

PROVERBS 16:16

My son, eat thou honey, because it is good; and the honeycomb, which is sweet to thy taste:

So shall the knowledge of wisdom be unto thy soul: when thou hast found it, then there shall be a reward, and thy expectation shall not be cut off.

PROVERBS 24:13–14

If any of you lack wisdom, let him ask of God, that giveth to all men liberally, and upbraideth not; and it shall be given him.

JAMES 1:5

For wisdom is a defence, and money is a defence: but the excellency of knowledge is, that wisdom giveth life to them that have it.

ECCLESIASTES 7:12

Thank You,
heavenly Father,
for the wisdom You have given to me.
I want to remain humble,
recognizing that You are the source of
any knowledge that I have.
May I be wise in the choices I make,
so that others can learn from me.
Amen.

Bible Readings for January

January 1 - LUKE 5:27–39, GENESIS 1–2, PSALM 1
January 2 - LUKE 6:1–26, GENESIS 3–5, PSALM 2
January 3 - LUKE 6:27–49, GENESIS 6–7, PSALM 3
January 4 - LUKE 7:1–17, GENESIS 8–10, PSALM 4
January 5 - LUKE 7:18–50, GENESIS 11, PSALM 5
January 6 - LUKE 8:1–25, GENESIS 12, PSALM 6
January 7 - LUKE 8:26–56, GENESIS 13–14, PSALM 7
January 8 - LUKE 9:1–27, GENESIS 15, PSALM 8
January 9 - LUKE 9:28–62, GENESIS 16, PSALM 9
January 10 - LUKE 10:1–20, GENESIS 17, PSALM 10
January 11 - LUKE 10:21–42, GENESIS 18, PSALM 11
January 12 - LUKE 11:1–28, GENESIS 19, PSALM 12
January 13 - LUKE 11:29–54, GENESIS 20, PSALM 13
January 14 - LUKE 12:1–31, GENESIS 21, PSALM 14
January 15 - LUKE 12:32–59, GENESIS 22, PSALM 15
January 16 - LUKE 13:1–17, GENESIS 23, PSALM 16
January 17 - LUKE 13:18–35, GENESIS 24, PSALM 17
January 18 - LUKE 14:1–24, GENESIS 25, PSALM 18
January 19 - LUKE 14:25–35, GENESIS 26, PSALM 19
January 20 - LUKE 15, GENESIS 27:1–45, PSALM 20
January 21 - LUKE 16, GENESIS 27:46–28:22, PSALM 21
January 22 - LUKE 17, GENESIS 29:1–30, PSALM 22
January 23 - LUKE 18:1–17, GENESIS 29:31–30:43, PSALM 23
January 24 - LUKE 18:18–43, GENESIS 31, PSALM 24
January 25 - LUKE 19:1–27, GENESIS 32–33, PSALM 25
January 26 - LUKE 19:28–48, GENESIS 34, PSALM 26
January 27 - LUKE 20:1–26, GENESIS 35–36, PSALM 27
January 28 - LUKE 20:27–47, GENESIS 37, PSALM 28
January 29 - LUKE 21, GENESIS 38, PSALM 29
January 30 - LUKE 22:1–38, GENESIS 39, PSALM 30
January 31 - LUKE 22:39–71, GENESIS 40, PSALM 31

Bible Readings for February

February 1 - LUKE 23:1–25, GENESIS 41, PSALM 32
February 2 - LUKE 23:26–56, GENESIS 42, PSALM 33
February 3 - LUKE 24:1–12, GENESIS 43, PSALM 34
February 4 - LUKE 24:13–53, GENESIS 44, PSALM 35
February 5 - HEBREWS 1, GENESIS 45:1–46:27, PSALM 36
February 6 - HEBREWS 2, GENESIS 46:28–47:31, PSALM 37
February 7 - HEBREWS 3:1–4:13, GENESIS 48, PSALM 38

Reading Through the Bible in a Year

February 8 - HEBREWS 4:14–6:12, GENESIS 49–50, PSALM 39
February 9 - HEBREWS 6:13–20, EXODUS 1–2, PSALM 40
February 10 - HEBREWS 7, EXODUS 3–4, PSALM 41
February 11 - HEBREWS 8, EXODUS 5:1–6:27, PROVERBS 1
February 12 - HEBREWS 9:1–22, EXODUS 6:28–8:32, PROVERBS 2
February 13 - HEBREWS 9:23–10:18, EXODUS 9–10, PROVERBS 3
February 14 - HEBREWS 10:19–39, EXODUS 11–12, PROVERBS 4
February 15 - HEBREWS 11:1–22, EXODUS 13–14, PROVERBS 5
February 16 - HEBREWS 11:23–40, EXODUS 15, PROVERBS 6:1–7:5
February 17 - HEBREWS 12, EXODUS 16–17, PROVERBS 7:6–27
February 18 - HEBREWS 13, EXODUS 18–19, PROVERBS 8
February 19 - MATTHEW 1, EXODUS 20–21, PROVERBS 9
February 20 - MATTHEW 2, EXODUS 22–23, PROVERBS 10
February 21 - MATTHEW 3, EXODUS 24, PROVERBS 11
February 22 - MATTHEW 4, EXODUS 25–27, PROVERBS 12
February 23 - MATTHEW 5:1–20, EXODUS 28–29, PROVERBS 13
February 24 - MATTHEW 5:21–48, EXODUS 30–32, PROVERBS 14
February 25 - MATTHEW 6:1–18, EXODUS 33–34, PROVERBS 15
February 26 - MATTHEW 6:19–34, EXODUS 35–36, PROVERBS 16
February 27 - MATTHEW 7, EXODUS 37–38, PROVERBS 17
February 28 - MATTHEW 8:1–13, EXODUS 39–40, PROVERBS 18

Bible Readings for March

March 1 - MATTHEW 8:14–34, LEVITICUS 1–2, PROVERBS 19
March 2 - MATTHEW 9:1–17, LEVITICUS 3–4, PROVERBS 20
March 3 - MATTHEW 9:18–38, LEVITICUS 5–6, PROVERBS 21
March 4 - MATTHEW 10:1–25, LEVITICUS 7–8, PROVERBS 22
March 5 - MATTHEW 10:26–42, LEVITICUS 9–10, PROVERBS 23
March 6 - MATTHEW 11:1–19, LEVITICUS 11–12, PROVERBS 24
March 7 - MATTHEW 11:20–30, LEVITICUS 13, PROVERBS 25
March 8 - MATTHEW 12:1–21, LEVITICUS 14, PROVERBS 26
March 9 - MATTHEW 12:22–50, LEVITICUS 15–16, PROVERBS 27
March 10 - MATTHEW 13:1–23, LEVITICUS 17–18, PROVERBS 28
March 11 - MATTHEW 13:24–58, LEVITICUS 19, PROVERBS 29
March 12 - MATTHEW 14:1–21, LEVITICUS 20–21, PROVERBS 30
March 13 - MATTHEW 14:22–36, LEVITICUS 22–23, PROVERBS 31
March 14 - MATTHEW 15:1–20, LEVITICUS 24–25, ECCLESIASTES 1:1–11
March 15 - MATTHEW 15:21–39, LEVITICUS 26–27, ECCLESIASTES 1:12–2:26
March 16 - MATTHEW 16, NUMBERS 1–2, ECCLESIASTES 3:1–15
March 17 - MATTHEW 17, NUMBERS 3–4, ECCLESIASTES 3:16–4:16
March 18 - MATTHEW 18:1–20, NUMBERS 5–6, ECCLESIASTES 5
March 19 - MATTHEW 18:21–35, NUMBERS 7–8, ECCLESIASTES 6
March 20 - MATTHEW 19:1–15, NUMBERS 9–10, ECCLESIASTES 7
March 21 - MATTHEW 19:16–30, NUMBERS 11–12, ECCLESIASTES 8

Light for My Path *for Grandparents*

Bible Readings for April

April 28 - ACTS 12, JOSHUA 15–17, JOB 28
April 29 - ACTS 13:1–25, JOSHUA 18–19, JOB 29
April 30 - ACTS 13:26–52, JOSHUA 20–21, JOB 30

Bible Readings for May

May 1 - ACTS 14, JOSHUA 22, JOB 31
May 2 - ACTS 15:1–21, JOSHUA 23–24, JOB 32
May 3 - ACTS 15:22–41, JUDGES 1, JOB 33
May 4 - ACTS 16:1–15, JUDGES 2–3, JOB 34
May 5 - ACTS 16:16–40, JUDGES 4–5, JOB 35
May 6 - ACTS 17:1–15, JUDGES 6, JOB 36
May 7 - ACTS 17:16–34, JUDGES 7–8, JOB 37
May 8 - ACTS 18, JUDGES 9, JOB 38
May 9 - ACTS 19:1–20, JUDGES 10:1–11:33, JOB 39
May 10 - ACTS 19:21–41, JUDGES 11:34–12:15, JOB 40
May 11 - ACTS 20:1–16, JUDGES 13, JOB 41
May 12 - ACTS 20:17–38, JUDGES 14–15, JOB 42
May 13 - ACTS 21:1–36, JUDGES 16, PSALM 42
May 14 - ACTS 21:37–22:29, JUDGES 17–18, PSALM 43
May 15 - ACTS 22:30–23:22, JUDGES 19, PSALM 44
May 16 - ACTS 23:23–24:9, JUDGES 20, PSALM 45
May 17 - ACTS 24:10–27, JUDGES 21, PSALM 46
May 18 - ACTS 25, RUTH 1–2, PSALM 47
May 19 - ACTS 26:1–18, RUTH 3–4, PSALM 48
May 20 - ACTS 26:19–32, I SAMUEL 1:1–2:10, PSALM 49
May 21 - ACTS 27:1–12, I SAMUEL 2:11–36, PSALM 50
May 22 - ACTS 27:13–44, I SAMUEL 3, PSALM 51
May 23 - ACTS 28:1–16, I SAMUEL 4–5, PSALM 52
May 24 - ACTS 28:17–31, I SAMUEL 6–7, PSALM 53
May 25 - ROMANS 1:1–15, I SAMUEL 8, PSALM 54
May 26 - ROMANS 1:16–32, I SAMUEL 9:1–10:16, PSALM 55
May 27 - ROMANS 2:1–3:8, I SAMUEL 10:17–11:15, PSALM 56
May 28 - ROMANS 3:9–31, I SAMUEL 12, PSALM 57
May 29 - ROMANS 4, I SAMUEL 13, PSALM 58
May 30 - ROMANS 5, I SAMUEL 14, PSALM 59
May 31 - ROMANS 6, I SAMUEL 15, PSALM 60

Bible Readings for June

June 1 - ROMANS 7, I SAMUEL 16, PSALM 61
June 2 - ROMANS 8 I SAMUEL 17:1–54, PSALM 62
June 3 - ROMANS 9:1–29, I SAMUEL 17:55–18:30, PSALM 63
June 4 - ROMANS 9:30–10:21, I SAMUEL 19, PSALM 64
June 5 - ROMANS 11:1–24, I SAMUEL 20, PSALM 65

June 6 - Romans 11:25–36, 1 Samuel 21–22, Psalm 66
June 7 - Romans 12, 1 Samuel 23–24, Psalm 67
June 8 - Romans 13, 1 Samuel 25, Psalm 68
June 9 - Romans 14, 1 Samuel 26, Psalm 69
June 10 - Romans 15:1–13, 1 Samuel 27–28, Psalm 70
June 11 - Romans 15:14–33, 1 Samuel 29–31, Psalm 71
June 12 - Romans 16, 2 Samuel 1, Psalm 72
June 13 - Mark 1:1–20, 2 Samuel 2:1–3:1, Daniel 1
June 14 - Mark 1:21–45, 2 Samuel 3:2–39, Daniel 2:1–23
June 15 - Mark 2, 2 Samuel 4–5, Daniel 2:24–49
June 16 - Mark 3:1–19, 2 Samuel 6, Daniel 3
June 17 - Mark 3:20–35, 2 Samuel 7–8, Daniel 4
June 18 - Mark 4:1–20, 2 Samuel 9–10, Daniel 5
June 19 - Mark 4:21–41, 2 Samuel 11–12, Daniel 6
June 20 - Mark 5:1–20, 2 Samuel 13, Daniel 7
June 21 - Mark 5:21–43, 2 Samuel 14, Daniel 8
June 22 - Mark 6:1–29, 2 Samuel 15, Daniel 9
June 23 - Mark 6:30–56, 2 Samuel 16, Daniel 10
June 24 - Mark 7:1–13, 2 Samuel 17, Daniel 11:1–19
June 25 - Mark 7:14–37, 2 Samuel 18, Daniel 11:20–45
June 26 - Mark 8:1–21, 2 Samuel 19, Daniel 12
June 27 - Mark 8:22–9:1, 2 Samuel 20–21, Hosea 1:1–2:1
June 28 - Mark 9:2–50, 2 Samuel 22, Hosea 2:2–23
June 29 - Mark 10:1–31, 2 Samuel 23, Hosea 3
June 30 - Mark 10:32–52, 2 Samuel 24, Hosea 4:1–11

Bible Readings for July

July 1 - Mark 11:1–14, 1 Kings 1, Hosea 4:12–5:4
July 2 - Mark 11:15–33, 1 Kings 2, Hosea 5:5–15
July 3 - Mark 12:1–27, 1 Kings 3, Hosea 6:1–7:2
July 4 - Mark 12:28–44, 1 Kings 4–5, Hosea 7:3–16
July 5 - Mark 13:1–13, 1 Kings 6, Hosea 8
July 6 - Mark 13:14–37, 1 Kings 7, Hosea 9:1–16
July 7 - Mark 14:1–31, 1 Kings 8, Hosea 9:17–10:15
July 8 - Mark 14:32–72, 1 Kings 9, Hosea 11:1–11
July 9 - Mark 15:1–20, 1 Kings 10, Hosea 11:12–12:14
July 10 - Mark 15:21–47, 1 Kings 11, Hosea 13
July 11 - Mark 16, 1 Kings 12:1–31, Hosea 14
July 12 - 1 Corinthians 1:1–17, 1 Kings 12:32–13:34, Joel 1
July 13 - 1 Corinthians 1:18–31, 1 Kings 14, Joel 2:1–11
July 14 - 1 Corinthians 2, 1 Kings 15:1–32, Joel 2:12–32
July 15 - 1 Corinthians 3, 1 Kings 15:33–16:34, Joel 3
July 16 - 1 Corinthians 4, 1 Kings 17, Amos 1
July 17 - 1 Corinthians 5, 1 Kings 18, Amos 2:1–3:2

July 18 - 1 CORINTHIANS 6, 1 KINGS 19, AMOS 3:3–4:3
July 19 - 1 CORINTHIANS 7:1–24, 1 KINGS 20, AMOS 4:4–13
July 20 - 1 CORINTHIANS 7:25–40, 1 KINGS 21, AMOS 5
July 21 - 1 CORINTHIANS 8, 1 KINGS 22, AMOS 6
July 22 - 1 CORINTHIANS 9, 2 KINGS 1–2, AMOS 7
July 23 - 1 CORINTHIANS 10, 2 KINGS 3, AMOS 8
July 24 - 1 CORINTHIANS 11:1–16, 2 KINGS 4, AMOS 9
July 25 - 1 CORINTHIANS 11:17–34, 2 KINGS 5, OBADIAH
July 26 - 1 CORINTHIANS 12, 2 KINGS 6:1–7:2, JONAH 1
July 27 - 1 CORINTHIANS 13, 2 KINGS 7:3–20, JONAH 2
July 28 - 1 CORINTHIANS 14:1–25, 2 KINGS 8, JONAH 3
July 29 - 1 CORINTHIANS 14:26–40, 2 KINGS 9, JONAH 4
July 30 - 1 CORINTHIANS 15:1–34, 2 KINGS 10, MICAH 1
July 31 - 1 CORINTHIANS 15:35–58, 2 KINGS 11, MICAH 2

Bible Readings for August

August 1 - 1 CORINTHIANS 16, 2 KINGS 12–13, MICAH 3
August 2 - 2 CORINTHIANS 1:1–2:4, 2 KINGS 14, MICAH 4:1–5:1
August 3 - 2 CORINTHIANS 2:5–3:18, 2 KINGS 15–16, MICAH 5:2–15
August 4 - 2 CORINTHIANS 4:1–5:10, 2 KINGS 17, MICAH 6
August 5 - 2 CORINTHIANS 5:11–6:13, 2 KINGS 18, MICAH 7
August 6 - 2 CORINTHIANS 6:14–7:16, 2 KINGS 19, NAHUM 1
August 7 - 2 CORINTHIANS 8, 2 KINGS 20–21, NAHUM 2
August 8 - 2 CORINTHIANS 9, 2 KINGS 22:1–23:35, NAHUM 3
August 9 - 2 CORINTHIANS 10, 2 KINGS 23:36–24:20, HABAKKUK 1
August 10 - 2 CORINTHIANS 11, 2 KINGS 25, HABAKKUK 2
August 11 - 2 CORINTHIANS 12, 1 CHRONICLES 1–2, HABAKKUK 3
August 12 - 2 CORINTHIANS 13, 1 CHRONICLES 3–4, ZEPHANIAH 1
August 13 - JOHN 1:1–18, 1 CHRONICLES 5–6, ZEPHANIAH 2
August 14 - JOHN 1:19–34, 1 CHRONICLES 7–8, ZEPHANIAH 3
August 15 - JOHN 1:35–51, 1 CHRONICLES 9, HAGGAI 1–2
August 16 - JOHN 2, 1 CHRONICLES 10–11, ZECHARIAH 1
August 17 - JOHN 3:1–21, 1 CHRONICLES 12, ZECHARIAH 2
August 18 - JOHN 3:22–36, 1 CHRONICLES 13–14, ZECHARIAH 3
August 19 - JOHN 4:1–26, 1 CHRONICLES 15:1–16:6, ZECHARIAH 4
August 20 - JOHN 4:27–42, 1 CHRONICLES 16:7–43, ZECHARIAH 5
August 21 - JOHN 4:43–54, 1 CHRONICLES 17, ZECHARIAH 6
August 22 - JOHN 5:1–18, 1 CHRONICLES 18–19, ZECHARIAH 7
August 23 - JOHN 5:19–47, 1 CHRONICLES 20:1–22:1, ZECHARIAH 8
August 24 - JOHN 6:1–21, 1 CHRONICLES 22:2–23:32, ZECHARIAH 9
August 25 - JOHN 6:22–59, 1 CHRONICLES 24, ZECHARIAH 10
August 26 - JOHN 6:60–71, 1 CHRONICLES 25–26, ZECHARIAH 11
August 27 - JOHN 7:1–24, 1 CHRONICLES 27–28, ZECHARIAH 12
August 28 - JOHN 7:25–52, 1 CHRONICLES 29, ZECHARIAH 13

August 29 - JOHN 8:1–20, 2 CHRONICLES 1:1–2:16, ZECHARIAH 14
August 30 - JOHN 8:21–47, 2 CHRONICLES 2:17–5:1, MALACHI 1:1–2:9
August 31 - JOHN 8:48–59, 2 CHRONICLES 5:2–14, MALACHI 2:10–16

Bible Readings for September

September 1 - JOHN 9:1–23, 2 CHRONICLES 6, MALACHI 2:17–3:18
September 2 - JOHN 9:24–41, 2 CHRONICLES 7, MALACHI 4
September 3 - JOHN 10:1–21, 2 CHRONICLES 8, PSALM 73
September 4 - JOHN 10:22–42, 2 CHRONICLES 9, PSALM 74
September 5 - JOHN 11:1–27, 2 CHRONICLES 10–11, PSALM 75
September 6 - JOHN 11:28–57, 2 CHRONICLES 12–13, PSALM 76
September 7 - JOHN 12:1–26, 2 CHRONICLES 14–15, PSALM 77
September 8 - JOHN 12:27–50, 2 CHRONICLES 16–17, PSALM 78:1–20
September 9 - JOHN 13:1–20, 2 CHRONICLES 18, PSALM 78:21–37
September 10 - JOHN 13:21–38, 2 CHRONICLES 19, PSALM 78:38–55
September 11 - JOHN 14:1–14, 2 CHRONICLES 20:1–21:1, PSALM 78:56–72
September 12 - JOHN 14:15–31, 2 CHRONICLES 21:2–22:12, PSALM 79
September 13 - JOHN 15:1–16:4, 2 CHRONICLES 23, PSALM 80
September 14 - JOHN 16:4–33, 2 CHRONICLES 24, PSALM 81
September 15 - JOHN 17, 2 CHRONICLES 25, PSALM 82
September 16 - JOHN 18:1–18, 2 CHRONICLES 26, PSALM 83
September 17 - JOHN 18:19–38, 2 CHRONICLES 27–28, PSALM 84
September 18 - JOHN 18:38–19:16, 2 CHRONICLES 29, PSALM 85
September 19 - JOHN 19:16–42, 2 CHRONICLES 30, PSALM 86
September 20 - JOHN 20:1–18, 2 CHRONICLES 31, PSALM 87
September 21 - JOHN 20:19–31, 2 CHRONICLES 32, PSALM 88
September 22 - JOHN 21, 2 CHRONICLES 33, PSALM 89:1–18
September 23 - 1 JOHN 1, 2 CHRONICLES 34, PSALM 89:19–37
September 24 - 1 JOHN 2, 2 CHRONICLES 35, PSALM 89:38–52
September 25 - 1 JOHN 3, 2 CHRONICLES 36, PSALM 90
September 26 - 1 JOHN 4, EZRA 1–2, PSALM 91
September 27 - 1 JOHN 5, EZRA 3–4, PSALM 92
September 28 - 2 JOHN, EZRA 5–6, PSALM 93
September 29 - 3 JOHN, EZRA 7–8, PSALM 94
September 30 - JUDE, EZRA 9–10, PSALM 95

Bible Readings for October

October 1 - REVELATION 1, NEHEMIAH 1–2, PSALM 96
October 2 - REVELATION 2, NEHEMIAH 3, PSALM 97
October 3 - REVELATION 3, NEHEMIAH 4, PSALM 98
October 4 - REVELATION 4, NEHEMIAH 5:1–7:4, PSALM 99
October 5 - REVELATION 5, NEHEMIAH 7:5–8:12, PSALM 100
October 6 - REVELATION 6, NEHEMIAH 8:13–9:37, PSALM 101

October 7 - REVELATION 7, NEHEMIAH 9:38–10:39, PSALM 102
October 8 - REVELATION 8, NEHEMIAH 11, PSALM 103
October 9 - REVELATION 9, NEHEMIAH 12, PSALM 104:1–23
October 10 - REVELATION 10, NEHEMIAH 13, PSALM 104:24–35
October 11 - REVELATION 11, ESTHER 1, PSALM 105:1–25
October 12 - REVELATION 12, ESTHER 2, PSALM 105:26–45
October 13 - REVELATION 13, ESTHER 3–4, PSALM 106:1–23
October 14 - REVELATION 14, ESTHER 5:1–6:13, PSALM 106:24–48
October 15 - REVELATION 15, ESTHER 6:14–8:17, PSALM 107:1–22
October 16 - REVELATION 16, ESTHER 9–10, PSALM 107:23–43
October 17 - REVELATION 17, ISAIAH 1–2, PSALM 108
October 18 - REVELATION 18, ISAIAH 3–4, PSALM 109:1–19
October 19 - REVELATION 19, ISAIAH 5–6, PSALM 109:20–31
October 20 - REVELATION 20, ISAIAH 7–8, PSALM 110
October 21 - REVELATION 21–22, ISAIAH 9–10, PSALM 111
October 22 - 1 THESSALONIANS 1, ISAIAH 11–13, PSALM 112
October 23 - 1 THESSALONIANS 2:1–16, ISAIAH 14–16, PSALM 113
October 24 - 1 THESSALONIANS 2:17–3:13, ISAIAH 17–19, PSALM 114
October 25 - 1 THESSALONIANS 4, ISAIAH 20–22, PSALM 115
October 26 - 1 THESSALONIANS 5, ISAIAH 23–24, PSALM 116
October 27 - 2 THESSALONIANS 1, ISAIAH 25–26, PSALM 117
October 28 - 2 THESSALONIANS 2, ISAIAH 27–28, PSALM 118
October 29 - 2 THESSALONIANS 3, ISAIAH 29–30, PSALM 119:1–32
October 30 - 1 TIMOTHY 1, ISAIAH 31–33, PSALM 119:33–64
October 31 - 1 TIMOTHY 2, ISAIAH 34–35, PSALM 119:65–96

Bible Readings for November

November 1 - 1 TIMOTHY 3, ISAIAH 36–37, PSALM 119:97–120
November 2 - 1 TIMOTHY 4, ISAIAH 38–39, PSALM 119:121–144
November 3 - 1 TIMOTHY 5:1–22, JEREMIAH 1–2, PSALM 119:145–176
November 4 - 1 TIMOTHY 5:23–6:21, JEREMIAH 3–4, PSALM 120
November 5 - 2 TIMOTHY 1, JEREMIAH 5–6, PSALM 121
November 6 - 2 TIMOTHY 2, JEREMIAH 7–8, PSALM 122
November 7 - 2 TIMOTHY 3, JEREMIAH 9–10, PSALM 123
November 8 - 2 TIMOTHY 4, JEREMIAH 11–12, PSALM 124
November 9 - TITUS 1, JEREMIAH 13–14, PSALM 125
November 10 - TITUS 2, JEREMIAH 15–16, PSALM 126
November 11 - TITUS 3, JEREMIAH 17–18, PSALM 127
November 12 - PHILEMON, JEREMIAH 19–20, PSALM 128
November 13 - JAMES 1, JEREMIAH 21–22, PSALM 129
November 14 - JAMES 2, JEREMIAH 23–24, PSALM 130
November 15 - JAMES 3, JEREMIAH 25–26, PSALM 131
November 16 - JAMES 4, JEREMIAH 27–28, PSALM 132
November 17 - JAMES 5, JEREMIAH 29–30, PSALM 133
November 18 - 1 PETER 1, JEREMIAH 31–32, PSALM 134

LIGHT FOR MY PATH *for Grandparents*

November 19 - 1 PETER 2, JEREMIAH 33–34, PSALM 135
November 20 - 1 PETER 3, JEREMIAH 35–36, PSALM 136
November 21 - 1 PETER 4, JEREMIAH 37–38, PSALM 137
November 22 - 1 PETER 5, JEREMIAH 39–40, PSALM 138
November 23 - 2 PETER 1, JEREMIAH 41–42, PSALM 139
November 24 - 2 PETER 2, JEREMIAH 43–44, PSALM 140
November 25 - 2 PETER 3, JEREMIAH 45–46, PSALM 141
November 26 - GALATIANS 1, JEREMIAH 47–48, PSALM 142
November 27 - GALATIANS 2, JEREMIAH 49–50, PSALM 143
November 28 - GALATIANS 3:1–18, JEREMIAH 51–52, PSALM 144
November 29 - GALATIANS 3:19–4:20, LAMENTATIONS 1–2, PSALM 145
November 30 - GALATIANS 4:21–31, LAMENTATIONS 3–4, PSALM 146

Bible Readings for December

December 1 - GALATIANS 5:1–15, LAMENTATIONS 5, PSALM 147
December 2 - GALATIANS 5:16–26, EZEKIEL 1, PSALM 148
December 3 - GALATIANS 6, EZEKIEL 2–3, PSALM 149
December 4 - EPHESIANS 1, EZEKIEL 4–5, PSALM 150
December 5 - EPHESIANS 2, EZEKIEL 6–7, ISAIAH 40
December 6 - EPHESIANS 3, EZEKIEL 8–9, ISAIAH 41
December 7 - EPHESIANS 4:1–16, EZEKIEL 10–11, ISAIAH 42
December 8 - EPHESIANS 4:17–32, EZEKIEL 12–13, ISAIAH 43
December 9 - EPHESIANS 5:1–20, EZEKIEL 14–15, ISAIAH 44
December 10 - EPHESIANS 5:21–33, EZEKIEL 16, ISAIAH 45
December 11 - EPHESIANS 6, EZEKIEL 17, ISAIAH 46
December 12 - PHILIPPIANS 1:1–11, EZEKIEL 18, ISAIAH 47
December 13 - PHILIPPIANS 1:12–30, EZEKIEL 19, ISAIAH 48
December 14 - PHILIPPIANS 2:1–11, EZEKIEL 20, ISAIAH 49
December 15 - PHILIPPIANS 2:12–30, EZEKIEL 21–22, ISAIAH 50
December 16 - PHILIPPIANS 3, EZEKIEL 23, ISAIAH 51
December 17 - PHILIPPIANS 4, EZEKIEL 24, ISAIAH 52
December 18 - COLOSSIANS 1:1–23, EZEKIEL 25–26, ISAIAH 53
December 19 - COLOSSIANS 1:24–2:19, EZEKIEL 27–28, ISAIAH 54
December 20 - COLOSSIANS 2:20–3:17, EZEKIEL 29–30, ISAIAH 55
December 21 - COLOSSIANS 3:18–4:18, EZEKIEL 31–32, ISAIAH 56
December 22 - LUKE 1:1–25, EZEKIEL 33, ISAIAH 57
December 23 - LUKE 1:26–56, EZEKIEL 34, ISAIAH 58
December 24 - LUKE 1:57–80, EZEKIEL 35–36, ISAIAH 59
December 25 - LUKE 2:1–20, EZEKIEL 37, ISAIAH 60
December 26 - LUKE 2:21–52, EZEKIEL 38–39, ISAIAH 61
December 27 - LUKE 3:1–20, EZEKIEL 40–41, ISAIAH 62
December 28 - LUKE 3:21–38, EZEKIEL 42–43, ISAIAH 63
December 29 - LUKE 4:1–30, EZEKIEL 44–45, ISAIAH 64
December 30 - LUKE 4:31–44, EZEKIEL 46–47, ISAIAH 65
December 31 - LUKE 5:1–26, EZEKIEL 48, ISAIAH 66